Basic Concepts in Music

Gary M. Martin

University of Oregon

Wadsworth Publishing Company, Inc., Belmont, California

1968

L. C. Cat. Card No.: 66–19273
Printed in the United States of America

Third printing: December 1967

Basic
Concepts
in Music

WADSWORTH MUSIC SERIES

Basic Concepts in Music by Gary M. Martin

Basic Piano for Adults by Helene Robinson

Basic Resources for Learning Music by Alice Snyder Knuth and William E. Knuth

English Folk Song: Some Conclusions, 4th edition, by Cecil J. Sharp (edited by Maud Karpeles)

Exploring Music with Children by Robert E. Nye and Vernice T. Nye

First Experiences in Music by Lyman C. Hurd, III, and Edith J. Savage

Five Centuries of Keyboard Music by John Gillespie

Foundations in Music Theory by Leon Dallin

Harmony and Melody, Volumes I and II, and *A Workbook for Harmony and Melody, Volumes I and II,* by Elie Siegmeister

Help Yourselves to Music by Beatrice P. Krone and Kurt R. Miller

An Introduction to Musical Understanding and Musicianship by Ethel G. Adams

Introduction to Music Reading by William Thomson

Keyboard Skills: Sight Reading, Transposition, Harmonization, Improvisation by Winifred K. Chastek

Music Essentials for Classroom Teachers by Robert Pace

Music Fundamentals by Howard A. Murphy with John F. Park

Music in the Education of Children, 2nd edition, by Bessie R. Swanson

Music Reading through Singing by Charles W. Walton and Harry R. Wilson

Planning Music in the Education of Children: A Personal Handbook by Bessie R. Swanson

Rhythm in Music and Dance for Children by Sally Monsour, Marilyn Chambers Cohen, and Patricia Eckert Lindell

Singing with Children by Robert and Vernice Nye, Neva Aubin, and George Kyme

Talking about Concertos by Antony Hopkins

Talking about Symphonies by Antony Hopkins

Teaching Music in the Secondary Schools by Charles R. Hoffer

Toward World Understanding with Song by Vernice T. Nye, Robert E. Nye, and H. Virginia Nye

Preface

This programed book is designed to help solve an old and persistent problem faced by both students and teachers in nearly any beginning music course - such as music theory, music education, or music appreciation. The problem stems from the fact that students arrive in these courses with widely varied backgrounds in music. Although most students will have had some exposure to basic concepts of music, many will have an inadequate understanding of them. Complicating the problem is the fact that the gaps in individual knowledge seldom coincide.

The purpose of this book is to provide each student with the particular knowledge he lacks in order to bring the class to a uniform minimum level of understanding from which the teacher may proceed. The book has been carefully written, tested, and revised to perform this function. A branching program tests the student's understanding of each concept before asking him to read an explanation of it. The student who can answer the "criterion question" for a particular concept moves quickly to the next concept. If he can't answer the question, he receives either a short review of the subject or a lengthy explanation - according to his self-determined need. Thus the student spends time only on the concepts he doesn't understand, working always at his own speed and at his own level of understanding.

Four particular features - which the author has found lacking in one or all of the other books designed to do the same job - have been incorporated into the organization of this text:

1. A wide background in the basic concepts of music. The study is organized in seven chapter units that cover the basic components of music notation; notational components of rhythm and melody; harmonic structure of basic intervals and chords; major and minor scales, chords, and keys; and the basic structure of music (e.g. phrase, motive, period, and binary and ternary forms).

2. A more interesting approach to programed learning. Although the concepts are presented in very small steps, as in a standard linear programed book, there are several alternate routes through the same material, each with a unique mode of presentation. The varying techniques used in explaining concepts and in questioning the reader are deliberately planned to avoid the "pall" effect, which researchers have found to be a serious drawback in many programed texts. Seemingly endless chains of frames presented in the same style, frames that are too large, too small, or too complicated, are

among the causes of the pall effect. The result of this effect is that students become bored or tired, lose interest, and stop learning.

3. Self-evaluation tests at the end of each chapter. Tests reinforce a student's knowledge and show him the areas he needs to review. They are used here for both <u>teaching</u> and <u>evaluation</u>.

4. Review indexes at the end of each chapter, and a subject index at the end of the book. The chapter index is combined with the test answers so the student can immediately clear up his confusion on test questions he missed.

Undergraduate college students who cooperated in testing this book expressed enthusiastic approval with such comments as the following:

> These chapters served as a very good review, as I found that I had forgotten a lot. . . . an interesting way for such a large class to become equated in musical knowledge in a fairly short time. . . .more a game than a chore. . . . The chapters have been interesting, and I like moving at my own pace. . . .

Music, of course, is an art medium that must be heard to be appreciated. The person who desires to broaden his understanding of music must become involved with sound. The best that this book (or any book for that matter) can do to further musical understanding is to provide information that gives greater meaning to the creation or perception of musical sound. Correct use of this text will certainly leave more time for actual student involvement with music.

I would like to express my sincere appreciation to Dr. Robert E. Nye and Dr. John M. Gustavson of the School of Music, University of Oregon, for their assistance during the preparation of the book as well as their willingness to make classes available for the experimental situations used to validate the book's format. Several staff members of the Teaching Research Division of the Oregon State Board of Higher Education also deserve thanks for their help in developing the program format.

Gary M. Martin

Contents

Introduction

Programed learning may be a new experience for you. Although the teaching-learning principles involved are probably as old as education itself, recent methods devised for making textbooks conform to these principles are proving to be both interesting and helpful to the reader.

This book employs principles of programed learning, and is properly called a "scrambled" or "branching program" text. The term "scrambled" has been used because the text cannot be read by turning pages in the usual manner. In fact, there are a number of unusual characteristics about the book. To begin with there are no page numbers as you know them. Instead, the book is divided into *parts*, each *part* being a small unit of instruction with a number. You will frequently find two such numbers on one page. These part numbers take the place of page numbers throughout the book. Another unique feature is that you do not read the book straight through from beginning to end. You read only the parts indicated in the instructions. For example, from part 26 you may be instructed to turn to part 21 to continue reading. When you finish reading each part it is, therefore, important to note where you read next. You have now reached the end of part 1.

Please turn to part 3.

2

Oops!!
You did not follow instructions, but fell into the habit of reading pages in consecutive order. You cannot do this in a programed textbook. Please return to part 1 and follow the directions.

Good. You have demonstrated your understanding of the first direction you will encounter in your study.

On certain pages, you will come to the caption *Use the Shield.* There is a shield attached inside the front cover of the book. When so directed you should use the shield to cover the page below the part you are reading. Complete instructions for its use are printed on the shield.

At frequent intervals in the book you will find criterion questions which present alternative answers designed to test your knowledge of some musical concept. Beside each alternative will be a part number. You are to select the answer you think is right and turn to the part indicated. There you will find whether or not your answer was correct. If it was correct, new material will be presented. If not, an explanation will follow. If you are unsure of the answer, or if you realize that your answer would be a guess, you are to choose the alternative that states "I'm unsure" – or words to that effect. You will then be directed to a detailed discussion of the subject. You should remember at all times that your basic purpose in reading this book is to gain an understanding of the basic fundamentals of music. Honesty with yourself about what you know and don't know is imperative, and guessing will only impede your progress.

When you make a mistake in the program, you may be asked to reread certain pages. Be sure to read them even more carefully the second time. When you miss a question, you will probably come back to it a second time to test your adjustment since the initial mistake.

Because music concepts build on each other, a complete knowledge of one area is essential to an understanding of the next. Therefore, at the end of each chapter you will find a SELF-EVALUATION TEST that will help you determine how much you have learned – and whether or not you are ready to go on to the next chapter. You will thereby have a chance to review any material that may still confuse you.

It is hoped that this will be an interesting and informative experience for you. Go to part 4.

1 / Basic Components of Music Notation

A musical sound is a fleeting experience. In order to retain such sounds for reproduction in the future, a system of notation has been developed, just as a system of writing was developed to record the spoken word. This chapter deals with the basic symbols and words that constitute the modern music notational system.

objectives

After completing this chapter, you should be capable of correctly identifying the following musical terms and their equivalent symbols when you see them.

1. A music staff and the great staff.
2. The treble-clef and bass-clef signs.
3. A bar line and a measure.
4. Whole, half, quarter, and eighth notes.
5. Whole, half, quarter, and eighth rests.
6. The highest and lowest notes in a musical passage.

You will also be able to identify the action specified by each of the following words or symbols that are used in musical notation.

1. Crescendo

2. Decrescendo

3. D.C. (da capo)

4. D.S. (dal segno)

5. Fine

6. Repeat sign:

Now go to the next part.

In the example below are six musical symbols, all of which are number-ed. Below the example are four alternatives. In three of the alternatives the symbols are listed in different orders.

Compare the numbers in the example with those in each alternative and select the answer that lists the symbols IN THE SAME NUMERICAL OR-DER AS THE EXAMPLE. Then turn to the part indicated. There you will learn whether or not your answer is correct. If you are not sure of the names of the symbols, choose alternative a. Remember – no guessing.*

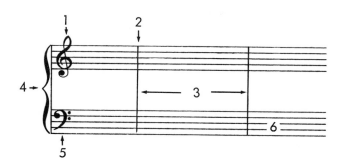

alternatives

part

a. I am unsure. Please explain this.		6
b. 1 – treble–clef sign	4 – great staff	
2 – bar line	5 – bass–clef sign	
3 – measure	6 – staff lines	15
c. 1 – bass–clef sign	4 – great staff	
2 – bar line	5 – treble–clef sign	
3 – measure	6 – staff lines	13
d. 1 – treble–clef sign	4 – staff lines	
2 – measure	5 – bass–clef sign	
3 – bar line	6 – great staff	17

*If you have already answered the question once, answer it again – correctly – and continue the program as directed.

You have helped yourself by stating frankly that you are not familiar with these terms. The following discussion will help you identify the six musical symbols.

Five lines placed together as shown on the right form a STAFF.

When two staves are used together they are called the GREAT STAFF.

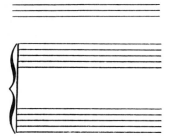

You now have two of the required answers. Lines in music are called staff lines. Five staff lines make a staff. Two groups of staff lines – that is, two staves – combine to make the great staff.

Use the Shield *

The five lines pictured here ⸻ are called _____ lines.

●

staff

If two groups of staff lines are joined together like this, the resulting figure is called a _____ staff.

●

great

Put the Shield Aside

On the great staff, special signs are used to designate the top staff, which is called the TREBLE CLEF, and bottom staff, which is called the BASS CLEF. The sign for the top staff looks like this: 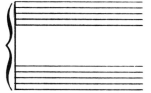 It is called the TREBLE-CLEF SIGN.

Perhaps you know that the male singer with a very low voice is called a BASS. The sign for the low staff--the BASS-CLEF SIGN-- looks like this: 𝄢

Go to part 7.

* If you forget how to use the shield read the instructions on it.

Use the Shield

When we use these signs in music notation we have a _____ staff with treble-clef and bass-clef signs.

●

great

The sign for the bottom staff is the _____ -clef sign.

●

bass

The _____ -clef sign identifies the top staff.

●

treble

This 𝄞 is called the _____ clef.

●

treble

The treble clef is the top staff, and the bottom staff is the _____ clef.

●

bass

When the treble clef and the bass clef are joined together like this, we have an example of the _____ staff.

●

great

Turn to part 8.

Use the Shield

The great staff is comprised of two staves. The top staff has this symbol 𝄞 and is called the _____ clef.

●

treble

The lower staff has this symbol 𝄢 and is called the _____ clef.

●

bass

Put the Shield Aside

The staff can be divided into sections by using vertical lines called BAR LINES. The distance between any two bar lines is called a MEASURE.

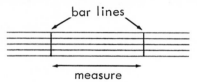

In the example below, there are three bar lines but only two measures.

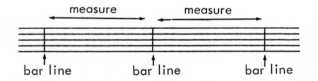

Use the Shield

This distance ▯▯▯▯▯ is called a _____ .

●

measure

A measure is the distance between two _____ _____ .

●

bar lines

Go to part 10.

You have made a small error. This was correctly called the great staff.

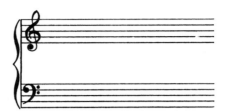

Go to part 10.

Use the Shield

A bar line is vertical, but five horizontal lines are called _____ lines.

⬤

staff

By putting this symbol (𝄢) on the staff, we can call it the _____ clef.

⬤

bass

The bass clef is the bottom staff and the _____ clef is the top staff.

⬤

treble

When the bass and treble clefs are put together as shown here they form the _____ _____ .

⬤

great staff

When two bar lines are drawn on the staff the distance between them is called a _____ .

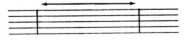

⬤

measure

Turn to part 12.

11

No, the treble-clef sign - 𝄞 - was CORRECTLY labeled in the example.

treble-clef sign ↓

Go to part 12.

---

12   *Use the Shield*

A staff with this symbol 𝄞 on it is known as the _____ clef.

●

treble

This symbol 𝄢 is used to designate the _____ clef.

●

bass

Both treble and bass clefs are divided into measures by _____ lines.

●

bar

The distance between two bar lines is called a _____ .

●

measure

Any staff can be divided into _____ by using two or more _____ _____.

●

measures, bar lines

Go on to part 18

You identified four of the symbols correctly, but two of your choices – the symbols for the treble clef () and the bass clef (𝄢) – were wrong. Please read the review that begins in part 14.

---

1. the great staff
2. the treble-clef sign
3. a bar line
4. a measure
5. the bass-clef sign
6. staff lines

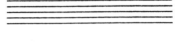
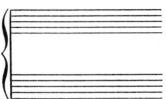

Five horizontal lines placed together as you see them on the right are called the STAFF, or STAFF LINES.

When two staves are placed together, they are called the GREAT STAFF.

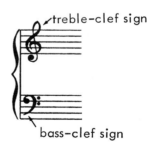

Special symbols are used on the great staff to differentiate the top staff, or TREBLE CLEF, from the bottom staff, or BASS CLEF.

treble-clef sign

bass-clef sign

The great staff is divided into sections by BAR LINES. The distance between two bar lines is called a MEASURE.

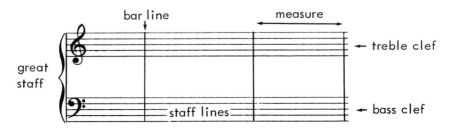

bar line

measure

great staff

← treble clef

staff lines

← bass clef

Now, return to the criterion question in part 5.

Right! The names of the musical symbols are given below. I'm glad you have identified them.

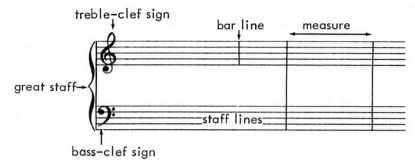

Having demonstrated that you know the basic framework for music notation, you are ready to consider some elements of musical meter.

Go on to part 16.

16

To refer to the relative duration of musical notes we will use the term TIME VALUE. A note's time value indicates how long it is held in relation to other notes. The most common time values are represented by the whole note, half note, quarter note, eighth note, and sixteenth note, which are shown below. You must identify them. Again, there are four alternative responses. After choosing your alternative turn to the appropriate part.

alternatives   part

    a. I'm not familiar with these time values.   20

    b. 1 – eighth note   4 – half note
         2 – quarter note   5 – sixteenth note
         3 – whole note   26

    c. 1 – sixteenth note   4 – half note
         2 – eighth note   5 – quarter note
         3 – whole note   23

    d. 1 – sixteenth note   4 – half note
         2 – quarter note   5 – eighth note
         3 – whole note   21

There seems to be something about this example that confuses you. By selecting this alternative, you indicated that you must have known something about music, or you would have chosen the alternative that stated "I'm unsure." For an explanation of the six basic symbols, turn to part 14.

Below are four musical symbols, one of which is labeled INCORRECTLY. Pick out the INCORRECT answer from the list and turn to the specified part.

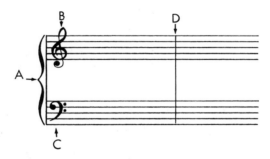

alternatives   part

    a. great staff   9

    b. treble clef   11

    c. bass clef   19

    d. a staff line   5

19

You have made an error. The bass-clef sign – 𝄢 – was CORRECTLY labeled in the example.

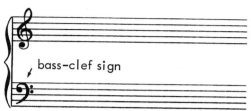

bass-clef sign

To clear up your confusion, turn to part 12.

---

20   It will take only a few minutes to explore the question. In arithmetic we have the following values, which you have seen a great number of times:

$$1/1 = \text{whole}$$
$$1/2 = \text{half}$$
$$1/4 = \text{quarter}$$
$$1/8 = \text{eighth}$$
$$1/16 = \text{sixteenth}$$

In music the notes are similarly named: whole, half, quarter, eighth, and sixteenth notes. The symbols for these notes are simply and logically constructed.

1. An elliptical circle is a WHOLE note: 𝅝

2. Put a stem on the whole note and it becomes a HALF note: 𝅗𝅥

3. Fill in the half note and it becomes a QUARTER note: 𝅘𝅥

4. Put a flag on the stem of the quarter note and it becomes an EIGHTH note: 𝅘𝅥𝅮

5. Put a second flag on the stem of the eighth note and it becomes a SIXTEENTH note: 𝅘𝅥𝅯

We now have the following symbols:

𝅝	=	whole note	𝅘𝅥𝅮 =	eighth note
𝅗𝅥	=	half note	𝅘𝅥𝅯 =	sixteenth note
𝅘𝅥	=	quarter note		

The duration of the whole note (𝅝) is four times as long as the duration of the quarter note (𝅘𝅥). The time value of the whole is therefore four times as great as the time value of the quarter note.

Go to part 22.

Congratulations, you have correctly identified whole, half, quarter, eighth, and sixteenth notes.   Turn to part 24.

Use the Shield

This (𝅝) is called a _____ note.

●

whole

The whole note has the (longest/shortest) time value in the example on the right.

●

longest

The note with the shortest time value in the example would be the _____ note.

●

sixteenth

It takes (how many) sixteenth notes (♬) to equal one whole note (𝅝).

●

sixteen

This note (♩) is a _____ note.

●

quarter

How many quarter notes does it take to equal one whole note?

●

four

This note (𝅗𝅥) is a _____ note.

●

half

Turn to part 25.

23

That example tripped you up. To find out why, turn to part 27.

24

There are times in music when brief silence, or a REST, is desirable. The symbols for the time values of rests are comparable to notes. That is, there are whole, half, quarter, eighth, and sixteenth rests. The whole rest is equal in time value to the whole note; the half rest is equal to the half note, and so on.

In the example below notes are paired with rests. All pairs except one contain symbols of equal time value. Find the UNEQUAL example and turn to the designated part. (A review of note values is in part 20.)

alternatives   part

a. I'm not sure I know the symbols for rests. Please
   explain them to me.   31

b. ♩ = 𝄽   34

c. ♪ = 𝄾   32

d. ♩ = ▬   30

e. 𝅝 = ▬   28

Use the Shield

It takes _____ quarter notes (♩) to equal one half note (♩)?

●

two

How many half notes does it take to equal one whole note?

●

two

If 1/1 stands for whole, 1/2 stands for half, 1/4 stands for quarter, and 1/8 stands for eighth, pick out the CORRECT example on the following staff. Under each note is a fraction, but ONLY ONE NOTE has the correct fraction value under it.

1/4   1/8   1/1   1/2

●

½ = ♩

Here's another example. There may be more than one correct answer.

1/4   1/1   1/8   1/2

●

1/1 = 𝅝 *, and ½ =* ♩

There were two correct answers that time. Now try this final example:

1/4   1/2   1/1   1/8

●

All four answers were correct this time. Were you?

If you failed to recognize them, review the material beginning in part 20.

If you were correct, turn to part 16.

26

The alternative you selected was incorrect. For an explanation go on to part 27.

27

Let's look at those notes again:

𝅝 – whole note

𝅗𝅥 – Add a stem and you get a half note.

𝅘𝅥 – Fill in the note and it becomes a quarter note.

𝅘𝅥𝅮 – Put a tail on it – we call it a flag – and it is an eighth note.

𝅘𝅥𝅯 – Put two flags on it, and it is called a sixteenth note.

If you were to add still another flag, what would you have then? . . . Of course, you would have a thirty-second note. (They are actually rather scarce.)

Now carefully choose the correct series below:

alternatives   part

a.
𝅝   𝅗𝅥   𝅘𝅥   𝅘𝅥𝅮   𝅘𝅥𝅯
1/1   1/2   1/4   1/8   1/16   16

b.
𝅗𝅥   𝅝   𝅘𝅥   𝅘𝅥𝅮   𝅘𝅥𝅯
1/1   1/2   1/4   1/8   1/16   20

You were asked to choose the INCORRECT response, but you chose a correct one: the whole note (●) and whole rest (▬).
Go to part 29.

Examine the chart below and make sure you know which notes are equal to each of the rests.

1.	whole note	●	=	▬	whole rest
2.	half note	𝅗𝅥	=	▬	half rest
3.	quarter note	♩	=	𝄽	quarter rest
4.	eighth note	♪	=	𝄾	eighth rest
5.	sixteenth note	♬	=	𝄿	sixteenth rest

If you would like a more detailed explanation, turn to part 31.
If you are sure that you can match all of the symbols in the above chart, turn to part 24.

30

Right! Assuming yours was an honest answer - not just a good guess - you are now ready to consider pitch determination. For that, turn to part 36.

31

When you know the time values of notes, the time values of musical rests are easy to learn.

The WHOLE rest carries the largest time value, and the HALF rest the second largest. These two rests look very much alike, as you can see in the example below.

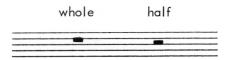

Here is a simple device to keep them from confusing you.

1. A whole rest (▬) is larger than a half rest in time value. Because it is larger (and therefore heavier), it hangs BELOW the staff line.
2. The half rest (▬) has a smaller time value than the whole rest. Because it is smaller (and therefore lighter), it sits ON TOP OF the staff line.

Thus, ▬ looks heavier, and so it is a whole rest. This ▬ looks lighter, and it is a half rest.

The next symbol (𝄽) is a quarter rest. Look at it carefully. The final symbols you need to recognize are the eighth and sixteenth rests. The eighth rest looks like this: 𝄾 . To make a sixteenth rest just add another flag to the stem of the eighth rest, thus: 𝄿 .

Can you guess how you would make a thirty-second rest? Add another flag to the stem. Thirty-second rest: 𝄿 .

To review briefly:

    ▬ = whole rest (below the line)

    ▬ = half rest (above the line)

    𝄽 = quarter rest

    𝄾 = eighth rest

    𝄿 = sixteenth rest

Go to part 33.

You were asked to choose an unmatched pair, but you chose the eighth note (♪) and eighth rest (𝄾), which are correctly matched. For a short review of this question, turn to part 29.

Use the Shield

This ▬ is a _____ rest.

●

half

The half rest is written (above/below) the line.

●

above

This 𝄾 is an _____ rest.

●

eighth

This 𝄽 is a _____ rest.

●

quarter

The whole rest is written (above/below) the line.

●

below

This ▬ is a _____ rest.

●

whole

The two rests 𝄽 and 𝄾 are _____ and _____ rests.

●

quarter   eighth

Go to part 35.

34

Instead of the incorrect response, you chose a matched pair: the quarter note (♩) and quarter rest (𝄽). For an explanation of your problem, go to part 29.

35

Of the rests 𝄽 , 𝄾 , and 𝄿 , which has the greatest time value?

●

quarter rest 𝄽

In the example on the right, only the _____ rest is correctly marked.

●

𝄾 = ⅛

In the next example, (how many) rests are correctly labeled. They are _____ .

●

two: ▬ = 1/1; ▬ = ½

All but the _____ rest are shown correctly in this final example.

●

last

If you made a mistake on this page, turn back to part 31.
If you made no mistakes, turn to part 24.

Music is made up of notes that vary in tonal range from high to low. Do you know how to distinguish the higher notes from the lower ones on the written page? From the example below pick out two notes – the HIGHEST and the LOWEST, in that order.

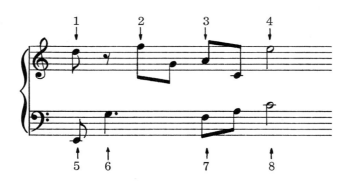

alternatives   part

    a. I'm not sure.   41

          high   low

    b.   1 and 8   37

    c.   1 and 5   42

    d.   2 and 5   39

37

That alternative was wrong. If you guessed at this answer you did yourself an injustice. Only legitimate mistakes are understandable. Unless you actually learn the material, it is of no value to go through the motion of reading it. Please read on in part 38.

38

On the staff below are a series of notes. The lowest note on the staff is the lowest in pitch. Conversely, the highest note on the staff is the highest in pitch. Moving from the lowest note on the left to the highest on the right, each succeeding note is graduated up in pitch.

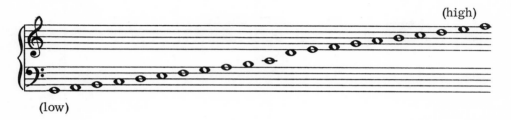

(high)

(low)

Which of the following notes is the highest? Which is the lowest?

1   2   3   4   5   6   7   8

alternatives

part

	highest		lowest	
a.	No. 1	and	No. 8	40
b.	No. 1	and	No. 3	41
c.	No. 7	and	No. 3	36

Good. You are now ready to learn the meanings of musical directions that frequently appear at the edge of the music staff.

Most of the terminology used in music is in Italian. Here are some of the more important directions:

1. FINE (pronounced fee-nay) – the end.

2. D. C. (DA CAPO) – go back to the beginning.

3. D. C. AL FINE – go back to the beginning and play to the end.

4. 𝄋 – a sign used to identify where you are to begin playing or singing.

5. D. S. (DAL SEGNO) – go to the sign 𝄋 .

6. D. S. AL FINE – go to the sign 𝄋 , and play to the end.

7. 𝄆 𝄇 This double bar with two dots is a repeat sign. When you encounter the SECOND double bar, you should return to the first one and repeat the passage between them.

Now turn to part 43.

40

Well, you still seem to be confused. You should be able to solve your problem by reading the explanation in part 41.

41

Just follow this one very simple rule: THE HIGHER THE NOTE IS ON THE STAFF THE HIGHER IT IS IN SOUND; THE LOWER THE NOTE IS ON THE STAFF THE LOWER IS ITS SOUND.

On the great staff, the pitch of the bass clef is lower than the pitch of the treble clef. When music becomes too low to be written conveniently on the treble staff, it is written on the bass staff. The illustration above is a good example of a melody using both staves.

Now, carefully find the highest and lowest notes in the example for the question in part 36.

No. You are right about the lowest note but your choice of the high-est was wrong. Turn to part 38.

———————————————————————————

In the two columns that follow, match the musical directions in column 1 with their proper descriptions in column 2 to choose your alternative.

1. D.S. (DAL SEGNO)   A. "go to the sign"

2. D.C. (DA CAPO)   B. "the end

3. FINE   C. repeat sign

4. ‖: :‖   D. "go to the beginning"

alternatives   part

a. I'm not sure   49

b. 1 = A
    2 = D
    3 = C
    4 = B   48

c. 1 = D
    2 = A
    3 = B
    4 = C   44

d. 1 = A
    2 = D
    3 = B
    4 = C   46

44

Not quite. It is easy to become confused about foreign words as you just have. For an explanation that will help you remember them, read part 45.

45

1. D. S. – DAL SEGNO (Notice the first initial of each word.) Segno is the Italian word for sign. The initials D. S. mean GO TO THE SIGN 𝄋 .

2. D. C. – DA CAPO (Notice the first initial of each word.) Capo is the Italian word for cap or top. The initials D. C. mean GO TO THE TOP, or, in other words, to the beginning.

3. Fine – end. Italians use this word as we use the word finish. The words AL FINE literally mean TO THE END.

4. 𝄆 𝄇 – repeat. When you see the second double bar (with the dots on the left side), you should return to the first double bar (with the dots on the right side) and repeat the music between the two.

Now choose the proper alternative below:

1. D. S. AL FINE: This means go back to the sign 𝄋 and play to the word fine. (Go to part 43.)

2. D. C. AL FINE: This means go back to the sign 𝄋 and play to the word fine. (Go to part 49.)

Molto bene! (That's Italian for VERY GOOD.) Now try another matching question, this time using dynamic markings, in part 47.

Dynamic markings determine how loud or soft the music should be. Dynamics in music are indicated by abbreviations for Italian words.

Below are two columns. Pick out the proper definition from the column on the right for each of the dynamic markings on the left and select the correct alternative below.

Markings	Definitions
1. pp (pianissimo)	A. loud
2. ff (fortissimo)	B. soft
3. p (piano)	C. very loud
4. f (forte)	D. medium soft
5. mp (mezzo piano)	E. very soft

alternatives   part

a. I'm not sure. Where is the explanation?   56

b. 1 = E
    2 = C
    3 = D
    4 = A
    5 = B   52

c. 1 = E
    2 = C
    3 = B
    4 = A
    5 = D   50

d. 1 = C
    2 = D
    3 = B
    4 = A
    5 = E   54

48

No. You have confused the repeat sign with the word FINE, which is the Italian counterpart of our word finish - or END. Go to part 45.

49

(If you came here from part 45, your answer was incorrect.)

If you understand the meanings of the Italian words, it will help you re-member how they are used in musical context. D. S. are the initials for the Italian words DAL SEGNO, which mean FROM THE SIGN. The sign referred to looks like this: 𝄋 . When you see D. S. you are supposed to GO BACK TO THE SIGN and begin playing at that point, thereby repeating the passage.

The second symbol was D. C., the Italian initials for the words DA CAPO. Capo is similar to our English word cap. The cap on a bottle is at the top of the bottle. Da capo also means THE TOP. In music it means GO BACK TO THE TOP, or GO BACK TO THE BEGINNING.

Now, for a review:
D. S. = "go to the sign"
D. C. = "go to the beginning"

The Italian word FINE (pronounced fee-nay) is related to the English HE word finish. It means simply STOP HERE, THE END, or THE CLOSING POINT after a repeat.

Use the Shield

If I were playing a piece of music on the piano and I came to the initials D. S. I would go to the _____ .

●

sign: 𝄋

If I came to the initials D. C. I would go to the _____ .

●

beginning

The initials ____ ____ instruct me to go back to the beginning and play from there.

●

D.C.

Go to part 51.

Very good! Hang on now, you have almost finished the chapter.
Turn to part 57.

The initials ___ ___ instruct me to return to this sign 𝄋 and
play from there.

●

D.S.

D. C. AL FINE means _____ .

●

Return to the beginning and play to the word fine.

Put the Shield Aside

Let's add our words together now:
1. D. C. al fine means: go to the beginning and play to the word fine.
2. D. S. al fine means: go to the sign 𝄋 and play to the word fine.
3. Although it isn't Italian, you must also remember this symbol:
𝄆 𝄇 (repeat sign). The arrows below show where you would go when you see a repeat sign.

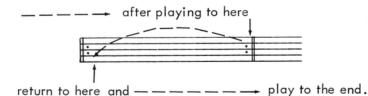

After playing without interruption to the second double bar with dots on
the left side, you would go back to the first double bar with dots on the right
side, and repeat from there to the end.

Turn to part 53.

52

You've confused two of the symbols. The explanation that should clear up the problem for you is in part 55.

53

Use the Shield

D. S. AL FINE means to go to the _____ and play to the end.

●

sign

D. C. AL FINE means to go to the _____ and play to the end.

●

beginning

FINE means the same as _____ .

●

end

This sign ‖: :‖ means that I should repeat the music that is found
(before/ between/ after) the double bars.

●

between

ORA PARLA UN POCO ITALIANO (which means, "Now you speak
a little Italian."

Return to part 43.

You have made a mistake, but the following explanation should help you understand these symbols.   Read on in part 55.

Each of the abbreviations – p, mp, mf, and f – is derived from an Italian word. If you can remember just three of the letters, the meanings of all of them will be easily understood.

p – SOFT   f – LOUD   m – MEDIUM

Therefore, if there are two f's (ff), the symbol would mean doubly loud or simply VERY LOUD. Conversely, two p's (pp) would mean doubly soft   or simply VERY SOFT. Put an m in front of either of them and it denotes moderation. In other words, mp means MEDIUM SOFT, or not quite so soft as p, and mf means MEDIUM LOUD, or not quite so loud as f.

That's all there is to it. Beginning with the softest sound on the left and going to the loudest sound on the right, we have the following series of symbols:

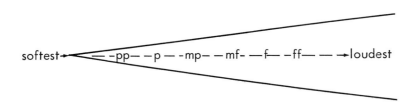

Study this example carefully. If you feel you need more exercise with the symbols, turn to part 56.

If you are ready to answer the original question correctly, return to part 47.

56

All of the abbreviations p, pp, mp, f, ff, and mf refer to various degrees of loudness or softness of musical tone. If you can remember the meanings of just three letters, the dynamic markings will be easy to understand.

p – SOFT   f – LOUD   m – MEDIUM

So, if you have two f's (ff), the symbol would mean doubly loud   or simply VERY LOUD. Two p's (pp) would mean doubly soft   or simply VERY SOFT. An m in front of either of them denotes moderation. That is, mp means medium soft, and mf means medium loud.

Progressing from the softest sound on the left to the loudest sound on the right, we have the following series of symbols:

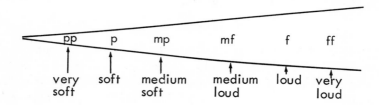

Use the Shield

The softest sound in music would be identified by using the letter ____ several times in a row.

●

p

When medium sound is desired (either medium soft or medium loud), the letter ____ is used with p or f to denote moderation.

●

m

"mp is louder than "mf"   (true or false)

●

false

The loudest sound in music would be identified by using the letter ____ several times in a row.

●

f

Go to part 58.

Do you know the meanings of the terms crescendo and decrescendo and their accompanying symbols, ⟨⟨⟨⟨ and ⟩⟩⟩⟩ ? One of them means to become softer, and the other means to become louder. The following statements are either true or false:

1. Crescendo means to become louder.
2. Decrescendo means to become softer.

alternatives

part

a. Both statements are true.   60

b. Both statements are false.   59

Use the Shield

Which of the following symbols means "medium soft"?

        p   mp   mf   pp

●

mp

Of the letters p, l, m, f,_____ does not have anything to do with dynamics in music.

●

l

Ranging from softest to loudest sounds, which of the following symbols are not in the correct order?

    softest   pp   p   mf   mp   f   ff   loudest

●

mf and mp are reversed.

Now return to part 47.

59

No, that was not the correct alternative. A look at the chart below should clarify the problem.

$$\overline{}\ \text{soft} \ldots \text{CRESCENDO} \ . \ \text{loud} \ . \ \text{DECRESCENDO} \ldots \text{soft}\overline{}$$

Crescendo means TO BECOME LOUDER, and decrescendo means TO BECOME SOFTER. Decrescendo has the same prefix (de) as decrease, and the word means TO DECREASE IN VOLUME OF SOUND.

Turn back to part 57.

60

Correct. The prefix "de" on decrescendo means to decrease the sound.

You have reached the end of Chapter one. The next step is to test and grade yourself to determine how well you have accomplished the objectives of this chapter. Turn to part 61.

Self-Evaluation Test

On the left side of this page is a column of musical symbols. At the right is a list of their names. Beside each number on the left is a blank. Match each of the symbols with the correct name, and record the proper letter in the blank by each number.

_____ 1.

_____ 2.

_____ 3.

_____ 4.

_____ 5.

_____ 6.

A. bass clef
B. bar line
C. great staff
D. measure
E. staff lines
F. treble clef

Match each of the following musical symbols on the left with its correct description on the right.

_____ 7.

_____ 8.

_____ 9.

_____ 10.

_____ 11.

_____ 12.

_____ 13.

_____ 14.

G. eighth note

H. half rest

I. whole rest

J. eighth rest

K. quarter rest

L. quarter note

M. half note

N. whole note

Turn to part 62.

All of the initials (or words) below are musical directions. Select from the right the proper English meaning for the musical directions on the left.

_____15. mf
_____16. f
_____17. mp
_____18. ff
_____19. p
_____20. pp
_____21. D.C. (da capo)
_____22. D.S. (dal segno)
_____23. fine

O. medium soft
P . very loud
Q. go to the sign
R . the end
S . loud
T . go to the beginning
U. very soft
V . soft
W. medium loud

Answer true or false.

_____24. The word "crescendo" means to become softer.
_____25. The word "decrescendo" means to become louder.

●   ●   ●

Now, check your answers with those in the key below, and grade your results thus:

22 to 25 correct answers: you have mastered the material.

21 or fewer correct answers: you need a review of the chapter. (You should be able to finish it much faster the second time.)

Regardless of your grade, IF YOU MISSED ANY QUESTIONS, it is important to review them immediately. The number of the part on which you can review a missed question is shown with the answer.

answers and review index*

1.	E	(staff lines) 6		14.	J	(eighth rest) 31ff
2.	C	(great staff) 6		15.	W	(mf) 56f
3.	F	(treble clef) 6		16.	S	(f) 56f
4.	A	(bass clef) 6		17.	O	(mp) 56f
5.	B	(bar line) 8		18.	P	(ff) 56f
6.	D	(measure) 8		19.	V	(p) 56f
7.	K	(quarter rest) 31ff		20.	U	(pp) 56f
8.	G	(eighth note) 20ff		21.	T	(D.C.) 49ff
9.	M	(half note) 20ff		22.	Q	(D.S.) 49ff
10.	H	(half rest) 31ff		23.	R	(fine) 49ff
11.	I	(whole rest) 31ff		24.	F	(crescendo) 59
12.	N	(whole note) 20ff		25.	F	(decrescendo) 59
13.	L	(quarter note) 20ff				

* Beside each answer, the subject of the question is shown in parentheses. The number of the part containing an explanation of the subject is on the right side of each column. The abbreviation ff means that the explanation begins in the part number shown and continues through following parts.

2 / Notational Components of Rhythm

Three of the most important components of music are rhythm, melody, and harmony. This chapter is primarily concerned with the first of these, namely rhythm.

In the preceding chapter, you learned to identify whole, half, quarter, and eighth notes and rests. You are now going to apply your understanding of time values to rhythmic concepts of greater complexity. Read the objectives carefully for a full understanding of what will be required of you at the end of the chapter.

objectives

When you reach the end of Chapter 2, you will be asked to do the following:

1. Recognize a definition of rhythm.
2. Identify various meter (time) signatures used in music.
3. Illustrate the number of notes and the kinds of notes called for in each of the meter signatures.
4. Match measures of music with their appropriate meter signatures.
5. Identify some of the various rhythmic possibilities in a measure of music.

Most of the above items relate to the meter signature and its use. You will also be asked to demonstrate recognition of these rhythmic features of music:

1. Two ways of writing eighth and sixteenth notes.
2. Tied notes and dotted notes, and the changes in note duration they cause.
3. Accents, Legato, and Staccato marks, pick up notes, and slurred notes. You should be able to match each of these terms with a proper description of its musical application.

It is good that you took the time to read the objectives. It is a demonstrated fact that we learn better when it is clear what will be expected of us.

Turn to part 64.

64

Rhythm has been defined as "the aspect of music comprising all the elements that relate to forward movement." Rhythm may more simply be called a "progression of pulses or beats through time." Anyone who has danced, or even tapped his foot, to music has experienced this feeling of movement through time, or – as it is called here – rhythm.

All but one of the following statements has something to do with rhythm. Which statement IS NOT CONCERNED with rhythm in music?

alternatives

part

a. The music of a waltz has a different beat than the music of a cha-cha.   72

b. Some pieces of music are performed much slower than others.   70

c. Some songs go too high for my voice.   68

65

That pattern was correct. Where did you slip up?

$$ \quad $$

An arithmetical breakdown will explain it. Since all four sections of the pattern are connected by equal signs, every section should be the time equivalent of every other section. The example above may be broken down as follows:

The four quarter notes (♩ ♩ ♩ ♩) equal the one whole note (𝅝).

The two half notes (♩ ♩) also equal the whole note (𝅝).

The eight eighth notes (♫♫ ♫♫) equal the whole note (𝅝).

This may also be expressed by saying that four quarter notes (♩ ♩ ♩ ♩) equal two half notes (♩ ♩), which, in turn, equal eight eighth notes (♫♫ ♫♫). Or,

$$ \quad $$

Now, return to part 71.

Correct. Let's try another, similar question to make sure you understand these relationships. Go to part 73.

First let's examine the individual notes under consideration:

𝅝 = whole note   ♩ = quarter note

𝅗𝅥 = half note   ♪ = eighth note

As you learned in arithmetic, it takes two eighths to equal one fourth. Similarly in music, two eighths equal one fourth – or one quarter note: ♪♪ = ♩ ; two fourths equal one half: ♩ ♩ = 𝅗𝅥 ; and two halves equal one whole: 𝅗𝅥 𝅗𝅥 = 𝅝 . Therefore,

1 whole = 2 halves = 4 quarters = 8 eighths

𝅝 = 𝅗𝅥 𝅗𝅥 = ♩ ♩ ♩ ♩ = ♫♫ ♫♫

You can change the order of these notes, or you can leave out an entire group between the "equal" signs; but you may not leave out any part of a group.

Correct 𝅗𝅥 𝅗𝅥 = 𝅝 = ♩ ♩ ♩ ♩

Incorrect 𝅗𝅥 = 𝅝 = ♫♫ = ♩ ♩

Use the Shield

Is the following example mathe-   𝅝 = 𝅗𝅥 𝅗𝅥 = ♪ ♪ ♪ ♪ ♪
matically correct?

●

No: either the last four notes should be quarter notes (♩ ♩ ♩ ♩)
or there should be eight eighths (♫♫ ♫♫)

Is this example correct?   ♪ ♪ ♪ ♪ = ♩ ♩ = 𝅗𝅥

●

yes

Go to part 69.

68

You are right. Whether a song is high or low has to do with melody, not rhythm.

As you learned in the preceding chapter, the basic notes in music are the whole note (𝅝), half note (𝅗𝅥), quarter note (♩), eighth note (♪), and sixteenth note (𝅘𝅥𝅯). It is just as true in music as in mathematics that two halves equal one whole, or that two quarters equal one half. For more on this, go to part 71.

69

Use the Shield

How about this one? Is it correct?   ♩ ♩ ♩ = ♪ ♪ ♪ ♪ ♪ ♪

●

yes

Here is one final example. ♪♪♪♪♪♪♪♪ = ♩ ♩ ♩ ♩ = 𝅗𝅥
Is it correct?

●

No: there should be either two half notes at the end (𝅗𝅥 𝅗𝅥) or one   whole note (𝅝)

Put the Shield Aside

By now, you probably realize that eighth notes can be written in two ways. A long series of eighth notes (♪♪♪♪♪♪♪♪) may be joined together like this (𝅘𝅥𝅮𝅘𝅥𝅮𝅘𝅥𝅮𝅘𝅥𝅮𝅘𝅥𝅮𝅘𝅥𝅮𝅘𝅥𝅮𝅘𝅥𝅮). They are frequently broken into groups (𝅘𝅥𝅮𝅘𝅥𝅮𝅘𝅥𝅮𝅘𝅥𝅮 𝅘𝅥𝅮𝅘𝅥𝅮𝅘𝅥𝅮𝅘𝅥𝅮) to make it easier to recognize the number of notes in the series.

Now, look at this pattern of notes.

♩ ♩ ♩ ♩ = 𝅗𝅥 𝅗𝅥 = 𝅘𝅥𝅮𝅘𝅥𝅮𝅘𝅥𝅮𝅘𝅥𝅮 𝅘𝅥𝅮𝅘𝅥𝅮𝅘𝅥𝅮𝅘𝅥𝅮 = 𝅝

If you think it is correct, turn to part 76.
If you think it is incorrect, turn to part 65.

That isn't quite right. Here's why. You must have noticed that some songs are slower than others. If you were to tap your foot to a slow piece of music and then tap it to a fast piece, you would see that the speed of the beat changes. That change is a change in rhythm. You were asked to select the response that is not involved with rhythmic differences. Now, see if you can't choose the correct response. Return to part 64.

The mathematical relationships of music notes is shown in the chart on the right below.

Observe the two ways of writing eighth and sixteenth notes shown in the chart – with flags or with connecting beams. There is absolutely no difference in time value between two notes with flags (♪ ♪) and the same two notes with a beam (♫).

Which of the following statements in music notation is mathematically accurate?

alternatives   part

a. o = 𝅗𝅥 𝅗𝅥 = ♩ ♩ ♩ ♩   66

b. o = ♩ ♩ = ♪ ♪ ♪ ♪   74

c. o = 𝅗𝅥 𝅗𝅥 = ♪ ♪ ♪ ♪   75

d. I need a clear explanation of these note values.   67

72

Woops, that one caught you. Why does the waltz have a different beat than the cha-cha? Because they have different rhythms. The waltz has a slow, simple rhythm in three beats, thus: 1 -- 2 -- 3 --. The cha-cha has a fast and complicated rhythm in four beats: 1 and, 2 and, 3 and, 4 and. Because of this difference in their beats, the two are rhythmically different - and you were asked to choose the statement that does not involve rhythm. You should be able to choose the correct response now. Return to part 64.

73

Which of the following musical equations is correct throughout?

alternatives   part

a. 𝅗𝅥 = ♩ ♩ = ♪ ♪ ♪ ♪ or 𝅘𝅥𝅯𝅘𝅥𝅯𝅘𝅥𝅯𝅘𝅥𝅯 𝅘𝅥𝅯𝅘𝅥𝅯𝅘𝅥𝅯𝅘𝅥𝅯   77

b. 𝅝 = ♩ ♩ = ♪ ♪ or ♫   79

c. 𝅗𝅥 = ♩ ♩ = ♪ ♪ ♪ ♪   81

d. I'm not really sure which is right.
   May I review this concept?   67

No, we must look at your answer again. The alternative you chose looked like this:

$$\mathbf{o} \ = \ \bj \ \bj \ = \ \eighthnote \ \eighthnote \ \eighthnote \ \eighthnote$$

When you break down its parts, you have:

          $\mathbf{o}$ is a whole note

          $\quarternote$ is a quarter note

          $\eighthnote$ is an eighth note

It takes four quarter notes to equal one whole note, thus: $\quarternote \ \quarternote \ \quarternote \ \quarternote = \mathbf{o}$; it takes two eighth notes to equal each quarter note, and eight eighth notes to equal one whole note. When all three values are expressed as a musical equation, you have this:

$$\mathbf{o} \ = \ \halfnote \ \halfnote \ = \ \quarternote \ \quarternote \ \quarternote \ \quarternote \ = \ \eighthnote \eighthnote \eighthnote \eighthnote \eighthnote \eighthnote \eighthnote \eighthnote$$

Now, compare this equation with the incorrect one at the top of the page. Do you see another way to correct the first one? Yes, it would be correct if the whole note ($\mathbf{o}$) at the beginning were replaced by a half note ($\halfnote$).

If you need further review, turn to part 67.

Otherwise, return to part 71.

75

You forgot something. Have another look at the alternative you selected:

$$\mathbf{o} = \boldsymbol{\mathit{d}}\,\boldsymbol{\mathit{d}} = \boldsymbol{\mathit{\flat}}\ \boldsymbol{\mathit{\flat}}\ \boldsymbol{\mathit{\flat}}\ \boldsymbol{\mathit{\flat}}$$

The first part of the example, $\mathbf{o} = \boldsymbol{\mathit{d}}\,\boldsymbol{\mathit{d}}$, is right; but in the second part eight eighth notes (or four quarter notes) are needed. Recall that $\mathbf{o}$ = whole note; $\boldsymbol{\mathit{d}}$ = half note; and $\boldsymbol{\mathit{\flat}}$ = eighth note. It therefore takes four eighth notes to equal EACH half note, thus:

$$\mathbf{o} = \boldsymbol{\mathit{d}}\,\boldsymbol{\mathit{d}} = \text{♫♫♫♫ ♫♫♫♫}$$

The combination of notes directly above is now mathematically correct. The group at the top of the page would be correct if it had eight eighths, or if the four eighth notes were replaced by four quarter notes (♩ ♩ ♩ ♩).

If you desire a more detailed explanation of these relationships, turn to part 67.

If the above explanation has clarified your problem, return to part 71.

76

You are right. The pattern is correct.

4 quarter notes = 2 half notes = 8 eighth notes = 1 whole note

With this understanding, you should be able to answer the criterion question for this concept. Turn to part 71.

Not quite. The pattern you chose looks like this:

$$\text{𝅗𝅥} = \text{♩ ♩} = \text{♪♪♪♪} \quad \text{or} \quad \text{♫♫ ♫♫}$$

The first three parts of the example are correct: $\text{𝅗𝅥} = \text{♩ ♩} = \text{♪♪♪♪}$

The last group of notes ♫♫ ♫♫ is incorrect.

These are eighth notes, just like the four notes in the third group. The flags have merely been written in a different way – that is, with a beam. In other words, ♪ ♪ and ♫ represent the same time value.
To be correct the pattern should look like this:

$$\text{𝅗𝅥} = \text{♩♩} = \text{♪♪♪♪} \quad \text{or} \quad \text{♫♫}$$

If you would like to review this concept further, turn to part 67.
If not, try that last question again by returning to part 73.

All that is new here is the dot after the note: ♩. Don't be misled by the fact that a dotted quarter note is used as an example. You can put dots after all other kinds of notes as well.
THE DOT INCREASES A NOTE'S TIME VALUE, OR DURATION, BY ONE HALF. The dotted note is of great importance in music because, proportionately, it is equal in value to two other notes. Can you identify the two notes that are the equivalent of a dotted quarter note?
Without guessing, choose the correct alternative below.

alternatives part

a. ♩. = ♩ + ♪   83

b. ♩. = 𝅗𝅥 + ♩   85

c. ♩. = ♪ + ♪   87

d. I'm not sure of the answer, but I am willing to learn.   80

79

Not quite. Let me explain it briefly. The pattern you chose looks like this: $\quad \half = \quarter\ \quarter\ = \beamed\ \ or\ \eighth\ \eighth$

The first two units are correct: $\half = \quarter\ \quarter$. The last two units – $\eighth\eighth$ or $\beamed$ – are incorrect. They are eighth notes and it takes four eighth notes to equal two quarter notes. To be correct the pattern should look like this:

$$\half = \quarter\ \quarter = \eighth\ \eighth\ \eighth\ \eighth\ \quad or\ \quad \beamedfour$$

If you need to review this concept further, turn to part 67.
If not, try the last question again by returning to part 73.

80

The concept of a dotted note is not difficult to comprehend. A dot is used to increase a note's time value. In fact, A DOT ALWAYS INCREASES A NOTE'S TIME VALUE BY ONE HALF.

For example:

Dotted whole note	= whole note	+ half note
𝅝.	= 𝅝	+ 𝅗𝅥
Dotted half note	= half note	+ quarter note
𝅗𝅥.	= 𝅗𝅥	+ 𝅘𝅥
Dotted quarter note	= quarter note	+ eighth note
𝅘𝅥.	= 𝅘𝅥	+ 𝅘𝅥𝅮
Dotted eighth note	= eighth note	+ sixteenth note
𝅘𝅥𝅮.	= 𝅘𝅥𝅮	+ 𝅘𝅥𝅯

Use the Shield

Which of the following notes has the longest time value? 𝅘𝅥. or 𝅗𝅥

●

𝅗𝅥 , a half note(𝅗𝅥) equals two quarter notes (𝅘𝅥 𝅘𝅥), whereas a dotted quarter note (𝅘𝅥.) equals a quarter plus an eighth (𝅘𝅥 + 𝅘𝅥𝅮)

Go to part 82.

Very good. You are progressing nicely. You are ready for the next concept – that of the dotted note. Go to part 78.

Use the Shield

A dotted eighth note (♪.) has the same time value as what two notes?

●

♪. = ♪ + ♪

What two notes would equal a dotted half note (𝅗𝅥.)?

●

𝅗𝅥. = 𝅗𝅥 + ♩

Is the following example correct?   𝅗𝅥. = 𝅗𝅥 + ♪

●

yes

Is this example correct?   𝅗𝅥. = 𝅗𝅥 + ♪

●

No: the last note should be a quarter note   ♩

Now, choose the correct response in part 78.

83

Good. The dot after a note increases its time value by one-half.
Hence, a dotted quarter note (𝅘𝅥𝅭) is equal in value to a quarter note plus
an eighth note (𝅘𝅥 + 𝅘𝅥𝅮). The dot is a handy device but sometimes it is
necessary to write in the note it represents. In music, the equivalent of the
mathematical plus sign is the TIE. For more on this subject go to part 84.

84

O.K. When you want to use two notes to equal a dotted note, you
TIE the notes in music notation (never use a plus sign). "Tied" notes are connected with a curved line, thus: 𝅘𝅥 𝅘𝅥𝅮 . Remembering that a dot after a note
increases its duration (time value) by one-half, choose the combination of
"tied" notes below that are the equivalent of a dotted quarter note.

This dotted quarter note (𝅘𝅥𝅭) equals:

alternatives   part

a.   91

b.   89

c. The two examples look about the same to me.
    Please explain the difference.   90

That wasn't a poor guess, was it? An honest mistake is permissable, but you should never guess.

The question was: What two notes does this note (♩.) equal? The dotted quarter note (♩.) is equal to one and one-half the value of a quarter note. In other words, it has the same duration as a quarter note plus an eighth note (♩. = ♩ + ♪). Remember, a dot after a note always increases the note's time value by one-half. Thus,

$$\mathbf{o.} \; = \; \mathbf{o} \; + \; \text{𝅝}$$

$$\text{𝅗𝅥.} \; = \; \text{𝅗𝅥} \; + \; \text{♩}$$

$$\text{♩.} \; = \; \text{♩} \; + \; \text{♪}$$

$$\text{♪.} \; = \; \text{♪} \; + \; \text{𝅘𝅥𝅯}$$

If you are ready to answer the criterion question correctly, return to part 78.

A more detailed review begins in part 80.

Woops! You need to read carefully the explanation of this question. It is in part 95.

87

Not quite. Here's hoping that wasn't a guess. An honest mistake is permissable, but you should never guess. The question was: What two notes does this note (♩.) equal? It is a dotted quarter note, and it is equal to a quarter note plus an eighth note ♩. = ♩ + ♪. Remember, A DOT AFTER A NOTE ALWAYS INCREASES THE DURATION OF THE NOTE BY ONE-HALF. For example:

$$𝅝. = 𝅝 + 𝅗𝅥$$
$$𝅗𝅥. = 𝅗𝅥 + 𝅗𝅥$$
$$♩. = ♩ + ♪$$
$$♪. = ♪ + 𝅘𝅥𝅯$$

If you are ready to try the question again, return to part 78.
If you need a more detailed review of dotted notes, go to part 80.

88

The explanation is simple.

In the above example the meter is six-eight. A piece of music is frequently said to be in six-eight time or six-eight meter.

Six-eight meter means there are six eighth notes (or their equivalent) in each measure.
Three-four meter means there are three quarter notes in each measure.
Four-four meter means there are four quarter notes in each measure.

In other words, the top number of the meter signature determines HOW MANY beats per measure, and the bottom number determines WHAT KIND of note represents the beat.

6 ⟶ how many notes per measure
8 ⟶ what kind of note

With this information, see if you can answer the question in part 93.

Correct! I'm glad you noticed that tied notes must always be on the same line or space. Otherwise they cannot be called tied notes.   These

notes 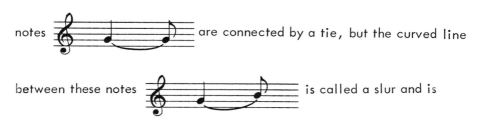 are connected by a tie, but the curved line

between these notes 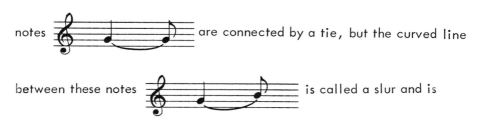 is called a slur and is

entirely different. (The slur will be explained at another point in the program.) The second note of two tied notes is never sounded separately. The first note is played and HELD for the duration of both notes without any break. As its name implies, the tie joins them together.

The next step of the program involves METER SIGNATURES. For that concept go to part 93.

Here is your explanation. There were two different curved-line symbols in the example.

slurred notes   tied notes

The slur extending between notes on two DIFFERENT lines in the first example does not combine time values and will not be discussed at this point in the text. Only when the two notes are on the same line or space are they tied.   In the example on the right above, the notes are joined by a tie and have a time value equal to a dotted quarter note (𝅘𝅥.). In the first example, the notes are not on the same line or space. Therefore, they are not tied notes.

equals   equals

Turn to part 92.

You have made a slight mistake. A dotted quarter note (♩.) is equal to a quarter note plus an eighth note (♩ + ♪). The curved line in the example on the right is called a SLUR, and does not combine the note values. ONLY WHEN THE NOTES ARE ON THE SAME LINE OR SPACE CAN THEY BE COMBINED BY A TIE. An example of a TIE is shown below.

slurred notes

these tied notes = this dotted note

If the notes are NOT on the same line or space (see the first example) the curved line has another meaning, which will be explained later.

If you need a more complete explanation of the tie, go to part 90.

Otherwise, return to part 84.

On the left side of this page are four examples of rhythmic combinations. For each, find the answer on the right that matches it in time value.

1. ♪.   A. ♩ + ♪

2. ♪ ♪   B. ♪ + ♬

3. ♩ ♩   C. ♩

4. ♩.   D. 𝅗𝅥

alternatives   part

  a. 1 = C
      2 = B
      3 = D
      4 = A   86

  b. 1 = B
      2 = A
      3 = D
      4 = C   95

  c. 1 = B
      2 = C
      3 = D
      4 = A   84

The meter signature* is found close to the clef sign – as illustrated below.

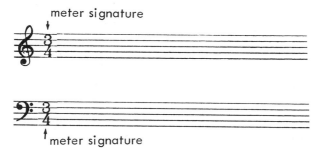

Meter signatures may consist of many different combinations of numbers. Some of the more common ones are $\frac{4}{4}$, $\frac{2}{4}$, $\frac{3}{4}$, $\frac{2}{2}$, $\frac{6}{4}$, $\frac{3}{8}$, $\frac{6}{8}$, and $\frac{9}{8}$.

Each of the two numbers in a meter signature has an important meaning. Select the correct meaning for each number in the meter signature from those below, and choose the alternative that corresponds to your answer.

In $\frac{3}{4}$ meter, the 3 determines _____ and the 4 determines _____ .

    (a) how many beats are in a measure
    (b) what kind of note represents the beat

alternatives

		part
a.	I really don't know. Please tell me.	88
b.	The 3 determines (a) The 4 determines (b)	96
c.	The 3 determines (b) The 4 determines (a)	94

* These are frequently called time signatures, but it is more correct to refer to them as METER signatures.

94

You apparently need to review this question.

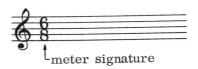

meter signature

In the meter signature pictured above, the number 6, on top, determines HOW MANY notes are to be in each measure. The number 8, on the bottom, determines WHAT KIND OF notes are the basis of the meter. Hence $\frac{6}{8}$ meter means 6 eighth notes (or their equivalent) per measure.

Likewise:

$\frac{3}{4}$ meter means: 3 quarter notes per measure.

$\frac{4}{4}$ meter means: 4 quarter notes per measure.

$\frac{3}{2}$ meter means: 3 half notes per measure.

$\frac{3}{8}$ meter means: 3 eighth notes per measure.

Now return to the criterion question in part 93.

---

95 You apparently need to re-examine the items in the last question. They are shown below.

1. ♪.	A. 𝅗𝅥
2. ♪ ♪	B. ♩ + ♪
3. ♩ ♩	C. ♪ + 𝅘𝅥𝅯
4. ♩.	D. ♩

The first item is a dotted eighth note, which is equal to an eighth note plus a sixteenth note: ♪ + 𝅘𝅥𝅯 , so letter C is its equal.

The second item consists of two tied eighth notes. A "tie" means to add the values together, thus: ♪ + ♪ = ♩ – D is its equivalent.

The third item consists of two tied quarter notes. By replacing the tie with a plus sign, we see: ♩ + ♩ = 𝅗𝅥 , so A is the correct match.

The dotted quarter note in number 4 is equal to a quarter note plus one half that value: ♩ + ♪ – B is its equivalent.

Now, see if you can choose the correct response for the question in part 92.

That's absolutely right. The top number in a meter signature determines HOW MANY beats will be in each measure, and the bottom number determines WHAT KIND OF note will represent each beat. If the meter signature is $\frac{3}{4}$, there will be three beats in each measure, and each beat will be the equivalent of a quarter note.

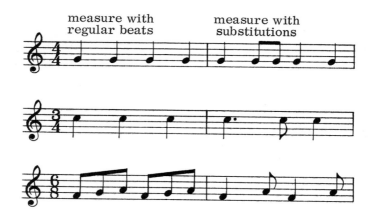

As you see in the last measure above, two eighth notes were substituted for one quarter note. This is a perfectly legitimate substitution, and such substitutions occur very frequently in music. For example:

Go now to part 98.

THREE-FOUR METER. You can determine this by finding out how many quarter notes are represented in each measure.

MEASURE ONE

We recently learned that a dotted quarter note equals a quarter plus an eighth ($\downarrow. = \downarrow + \eighthnote$). So, if we substitute an eighth note for the dot, the measure equals $\downarrow + \eighthnote + \eighthnote + \downarrow$, or the equivalent of three quarter notes. Thus, three-four meter is indicated.

When determining meter, it is necessary to find out how many basic beats are in the measure. The most common basic beat is a quarter note, although eighth notes are also used. By finding out how many quarter notes are in each measure you will be on the road to determining meter.

measure with the basic beat only   same meter with substitutions included

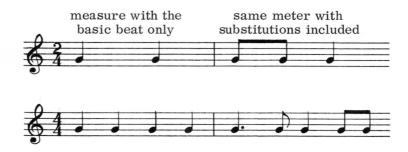

If you would like more practice with meter signatures, turn to part 104.
If not, answer the question in part 98.

Below are three musical examples with several substitutions in every measure. Can you determine the meter signature needed for each of the examples? Choose your answers from the signatures listed at the right.

1. 

2. 

3. 

Signatures

$\frac{3}{2}$ meter

$\frac{2}{4}$ meter

$\frac{4}{4}$ meter

Choose your answers and select the alternative below that matches your choice. Turn to the part indicated.

alternatives

	part
a. I know this step of the program is very important, and I am somewhat confused. I need a more detailed discussion.	104
b. 1 = $\frac{4}{4}$ meter 2 = $\frac{3}{2}$ meter 3 = $\frac{2}{4}$ meter	101
c. 1 = $\frac{2}{4}$ meter 2 = $\frac{3}{2}$ meter 3 = $\frac{4}{4}$ meter	99
d. 1 = $\frac{3}{2}$ meter 2 = $\frac{4}{4}$ meter 3 = $\frac{2}{4}$ meter	103

99

You've made a mistake, but we can now try to clear the matter up. Go on to part 100.

100

The first example looked like this:

What is its meter? $\frac{3}{2} - \frac{2}{4} - $ or $ - \frac{4}{4}$

The first note in measure 1 is a half note. A half note is equal to two quarter notes. The next two notes are eighth notes, and when combined, they equal one quarter note. The final note in the first measure is a quarter note. When all of these notes are totaled, the measure has the equivalent of 4 quarter notes in it, indicating four-four meter.

In the second measure, the 4 eighth notes have the same time value as two quarter notes. There are also two quarter notes in the measure, bringing the total once again to 4 quarter notes, or four-four meter.

What would the meter of this example be?

For the answer, turn to part 97.

Right. You have taken a successful step toward the completion of this chapter by correctly identifying those meter signatures. Let's try another similar problem to double-check your understanding of the important concept of meter. Go to part 102.

Determine the proper meter signature for each of the following examples, and select the corresponding alternative from those given below.

alternatives   part

a. If I am really honest with myself, I think
   a review is necessary for me to understand
   this question.   104

b. $1 = \frac{4}{4}$; $2 = \frac{3}{4}$; $3 = \frac{4}{4}$ 107

c. $1 = \frac{3}{4}$; $2 = \frac{6}{8}$; $3 = \frac{4}{4}$ 109

d. $1 = \frac{3}{4}$; $2 = \frac{2}{4}$; $3 = \frac{6}{8}$ 105

103

You have not selected the proper alternative. To clear up the problem read carefully the material in part 100.

104

Fine, let's consider the matter a minute. Beside the clef sign on the staff below is a meter signature.

The bottom number of the meter signature determines WHAT KIND of note will be the basic beat of the measure. In three-four meter, for example, the basic beat will be the quarter note.

The top number determines HOW MANY of these notes will be represented in each measure. Music in $\frac{3}{4}$ meter will have the equivalent of three quarter notes in each measure. In short,

$\frac{3}{4}$ meter = 3 quarter notes per measure.

$\frac{6}{8}$ meter = 6 eighth notes per measure.

$\frac{4}{4}$ meter = 4 quarter notes per measure.

$\frac{3}{2}$ meter = 3 half notes per measure.

$\frac{9}{8}$ meter = 9 eighth notes per measure.

Go to part 106.

That was not quite right. For an explanation of this question, go to part 108.

Use the Shield

With this meter signature there will be (how many) eighth notes in each measure.

six

With this meter signature there will be (how many) (what kind) notes per measure.

three eighth notes

With this meter signature the basic beat of the measure will be the _____ note.

quarter

With this meter signature there will be (number) _____ (kind) notes per measure.

●

five eighth notes

Turn to part 110.

107

You need to take another look at the question. Read the explanation in part 108.

108

The three examples were:

Each measure in this example has
the equal of 3 quarter notes: meter signature: $\frac{3}{4}$

This example has the equivalent of
6 eighth notes per measure: meter signature: $\frac{6}{8}$

There is the equivalent of 4 quarter
notes per measure in this example: meter signature: $\frac{4}{4}$

If you are still the least bit unsure, read the complete review in part 104.

If not, choose the correct response for the question in part 102.

Excellent. The next question will test your understanding of meter in a slightly different way. Turn to part 115.

Use the Shield

With this meter signature, there would be (how many) eighth notes per measure.

●

nine

The staff at the left is an example of _____ meter.

●

$\frac{3}{4}$ (*3 quarter notes per measure*)

This staff is an example of _____ meter.

●

$\frac{2}{4}$ (*2 quarter notes per measure*)

Here is an example of _____ meter.

●

$\frac{6}{8}$ (*6 eighth notes per measure*)

This staff represents _____ meter.

●

$\frac{4}{4}$ (*4 quarter notes per measure*)

Turn to part 111.

111

Use the Shield

A quarter note is equal to _____ eighth notes.

●

two

It takes _____ eighth notes to equal one half note.

●

four

This figure (♩. ♪) is equal in time value to _____ quarter notes.

●

two (because the dot and the eighth note take the place of the
second quarter note)

Put the Shield Aside

When a meter signature designates that a measure is in three-four meter, we have the following possible simple construction:

1   2   3   1   2   3   1   2   3

Many variations are also possible. For example,

is equally acceptable because the two eighth notes at the end are equal in time value to one quarter note. Likewise, this example is acceptable:

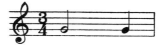

The half note at the beginning of the measure is equal to two quarter notes, bringing the total to three quarter notes, as required. A dotted note may also be used:

Continue in part 112.

As was determined earlier in the program, the dotted quarter note is equal to a quarter note plus an eighth note, the dot being equal to an eighth note. Hence the measure is once again brought to a total of three beats.

Each of the measures in the following example contains three beats. Examine them carefully and locate all three beats in each measure.

Use the Shield

Does the following measure have the correct number of beats?

●

no (there is an extra eighth note)

Does this measure have the correct number of beats?

●

yes

Which measure below is INCORRECT?

●

measure 3 (it needs another eighth note)

Go on to part 113.

113

Which of the following measures is INCORRECT?

●

measure 1 (it has one eighth note too many)

Put the Shield Aside

Let's determine the meter signature for these measures of music:

The first four notes in measure 1 are eighth notes. Each pair of eighth notes equals one quarter note. The meter therefore seems to be three-four. In measure 2 the dotted quarter note equals a quarter note plus an eighth note. When it is combined with the other eighth notes, we arrive at three-four meter again.

At first glance, you might think it difficult to determine the meter signature for the example below, but it is relatively easy.

The first two notes in the measure are eighth notes. Together they equal one quarter note. The next four notes are sixteenth notes - because of the double beam on their stems. Four sixteenth notes also equal one quarter note. Each pair of eighth notes at the end of the measure is like the one at the start. Each equals one quarter note. Thus, the measure has the equivalence of four quarter notes, as in four-four meter.

Go on to part 114.

Use the Shield

Below are a musical sample and three meter signatures. Which signature is the correct one for this music?

●

4
4

Which signature belongs with the next sample?

●

3
4

Which signature is the correct one here?

●

4
4

Are there any mistakes in the next example? Where?

●

no mistakes

Return to the question in part 98.

115

The meter signature in the example below is $\frac{3}{8}$. There should be the equivalent of three eighth notes in each measure. Which measure is not correct?

alternatives

part

   a. Measure 1 is incorrect.   118

   b. Measure 2 is incorrect.   124

   c. Measure 3 is incorrect.   122

   d. Measure 4 is incorrect.   120

You didn't choose the correct response. To learn why, go to part 117.

You were to choose the measure with a mistake in it:

Measure 1 has a quarter rest, an eighth rest, and an eighth note, in that order. The combined time value of the eighth rest and the eighth note is equal to a quarter note. Thus, the measure has a quarter rest followed by the equivalent of a quarter note. This indicates two-four meter.

Measure 2 has this pattern: ♫ ♫ (an eighth note connected with two sixteenth notes, followed by two eighth notes, also connected). The two sixteenth notes equal the time value of one eighth note. Therefore, the measure has the time value of four eighth notes or two quarter notes. The meter indicated is again two-four.

Measure 3 has an eighth note, a sixteenth note, and a quarter note. The last note in the measure is the quarter note, but the first two notes in the measure (♪ ♪) are NOT the equivalent of another quarter note. One sixteenth note is missing. Therefore, the mistake is in measure 3.

Now, try the question again in part 115.

118

That was incorrect. You will find an explanation of this question in part 123.

119

Each example below has one incomplete measure. In which example is the incomplete measure acceptable?

alternatives

		part
a.	Example 1	128
b.	Example 2	131
c.	Example 3	130

That alternative can't be right. When you add a quarter note and an eighth note, you have the equivalent of three eighth notes - or just what the meter signature called for. For a complete explanation go to part 123.

You have now reached the last criterion question in this chapter. To answer it correctly, please read it carefully.

In the three columns below, the first lists musical terms; the second shows the musical symbols used in their places; and the third column defines the symbols.

Match the three columns (your answer will be something like A-1-X or B-2-Y) and find your answer in the alternatives below.

Musical Terms	Symbols	Explanations
A. staccato	1.	W. separate the notes
B. tenuto	2.	X. lengthen the note
C. slur	3.	Y. stress this note
D. accent	4.	Z. connect the notes

alternatives

		part
a.	These words are strange to me. I would like an explanation.	125
b.	A-3-W B-2-X C-1-Z D-4-Y	127
c.	A-3-W B-4-Y C-1-X D-2-Z	132

122

You have made a simple mistake, but it isn't enough to be overly worried about. Let's study it for a minute in part 123.

123

The meter was $\frac{3}{8}$. Any combination of notes equal to three eighth notes would be correct. You were to find the incorrect measure.

Measure 1 has this pattern: ♩♫ ♪ (an eighth note and two sixteenth notes connected together, followed by an eighth note.) The two sixteenth notes are equal to one eighth note. When totaled, the measure contains the equivalent of three eighth notes. It is therefore correct.

In measure 2, this pattern is found: ♩. ♪ (a dotted quarter note followed by a sixteenth note). The quarter note equals two eighth notes, and the dot after it equals a third eighth note. There is a sixteenth note left in the measure which is not needed; the measure is, therefore, incorrect. It has one sixteenth note too many.

Measure 3 has the following note pattern: ♫ ♫ ♫ (six sixteenth notes). Each pair of sixteenth notes equals one eighth note. The six sixteenth notes equal three eighth notes, and the measure is complete and correct.

Measure 4 contains one quarter note and one eighth note: ♩ ♪ The quarter note equals two eighth notes, and the last note in the measure is the third eighth note. The measure is correct as it stands.

Now let's see if you can find the mistake in the musical example that follows:

alternatives   part

Measure 1 has the mistake.   126

Measure 2 has the mistake.   116

Measure 3 has the mistake.   115

Correct! You are doing very well. In fact you don't have much further to go in this chapter. Take a deep breath so your mind is sharp and
clear. Then answer the question in part 119.

Here is an explanation.

1. Staccato: This term is applied to notes that are to be shortened
   slightly, so that the tones are separated from each other.

 staccato notes

2. Tenuto: This term is applied to notes that are to be lengthened
   slightly. The mark is merely a line above the note, showing
   that the tone should be stretched out somewhat.

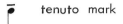 tenuto mark

3. Slur: This symbol connects a series of notes. It serves basically
   the same purpose as the tenuto mark, but it is used when more
   than one tone is to be lengthened.

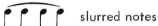 slurred notes

4. Accent: An accent mark is used when one note is to be played
   or sung louder than the others around it.

 accented note

Now return to part 121.

126

This question caused you some trouble, didn't it? Read the explanation in part 117.

127

That's right!

1. Staccato notes (♩̇ ♩̇) are to be separated from each other.

2. Tenuto notes (♩̄) are to be lengthened slightly.

3. Slurred notes (♩ ♩ ♩ ♩) are to be connected. If only two notes are involved (♩ ♩), they will be different tones. Otherwise they would be TIED notes.

4. Accented notes (♩̂) are to be stressed or emphasized more than the notes around them.

Congratulations. You are now at the end of Chapter 2 and ready for the Self-Evaluation Test. Your score on the test will tell you how well you have mastered the material.

Go to part 133.

You have made a mistake, so let's reconsider the question. Go to part 129.

You were asked to show where an incomplete measure is acceptable: in the first measure of a piece, anywhere in the middle, or at the end of a piece.
    INCOMPLETE MEASURES ARE ACCEPTABLE ONLY AT THE BEGINNING OF A PIECE OF MUSIC AND AT THE END OF A PIECE THAT BEGINS WITH AN INCOMPLETE MEASURE. The notes in those incomplete measures that begin a piece are called PICKUP NOTES. Many well known songs have pickup notes in them. Look at "Dixie" for example:

Another example of a pickup note is the beginning of the well known song "Auld Lang Syne":

Now, return to part 119.

You are right! An incomplete measure is allowed at the beginning of a piece of music. The extra notes are called PICKUP notes. One well-known example is our national anthem which begins with two pickup notes on the word "Oh."

Oh ___ say can you see. . . .

Although incomplete measures are permitted at the beginning of a piece of music, they are never permitted in the middle. In fact, to make all measures equal, the extra beat of the pickup note is usually borrowed from the last measure.

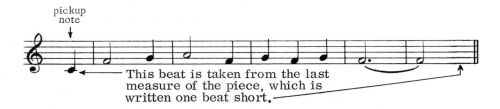

This beat is taken from the last measure of the piece, which is written one beat short.

Now   go to part 121.

You chose the wrong alternative but we can clear this up very quickly. Please turn to the explanation in part 129.

Not quite. Let's see why.

1. The staccato mark above a note is a dot (𝄐 𝄐 𝄐). Staccato marks are used to show that the notes should be separated from each other. Therefore the duration of tone is shortened very slightly.

2. A tenuto mark is just the opposite of a staccato mark (𝄐 𝄐). As the line above the note indicates, its tone should be stretched out, or increased slightly in length.

3. Slurred notes are basically the same as tenuto notes. The slur is used when you have many notes to connect, whereas the tenuto mark is used when there is only one note to lengthen.

   𝄐 𝄐 𝄐 𝄐   slurred notes

4. An accented note (𝄐) is to be played louder, or with more emphasis than the surrounding notes.

Return to part 121.

133

Self-Evaluation Test

On the left side of this page are nine musical symbols or word descriptions. At the right are eleven responses, lettered A through K, from which you are to choose the best description for each of the numbered items. Write the proper letter in the blank by each number on the left.

_____1. bass clef with meter signature

_____2. $\frac{2}{4}$ meter

_____3. ♫

_____4. rhythm

_____5. $\frac{3}{2}$ meter

_____6. ♫

_____7. treble clef with meter signature

_____8. $\frac{6}{4}$ meter

_____9. $\frac{6}{8}$ meter

A. 6 eighth notes per measure

B. same as ♫

C. (bass clef notation)

D. 4 half notes per measure

E. (treble clef with 6/8)

F. 2 quarter notes per measure

G. same as ♪♪

H. 3 half notes per measure

I. (bass clef with 3/4)

J. progression of pulses through time

K. 6 quarter notes per measure

On the left are a series of dotted notes and tied notes. On the right, the mathematical equivalents of each example are listed randomly. Select a letter for each number and write it in the proper blank.

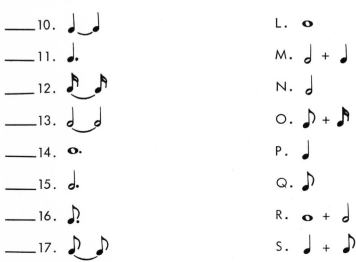

_____10. ♩‿♩

_____11. ♩.

_____12. ♪ ♪

_____13. ♩‿♩

_____14. o.

_____15. ♩.

_____16. ♪

_____17. ♪‿♪

L. o

M. ♩ + ♩

N. ♩

O. ♪ + ♪

P. ♩

Q. ♪

R. o + ♩

S. ♩ + ♪

Go on to part 134.

For the six music examples below, choose the proper meter signature shown at the right   and record your answer.

_____ 18.

$\frac{3}{8}$

_____ 19.

$\frac{2}{4}$

$\frac{4}{4}$

_____ 20.

$\frac{6}{8}$

_____ 21.

$\frac{3}{4}$

$\frac{6}{4}$

_____ 22.

_____ 23.

Match the examples on the left with the proper definition and/or name from the right.

_____ 24.

_____ 25.

_____ 26.

_____ 27.

_____ 28.

_____ 29.

_____ 30.

T. slurred quarter notes –
    to be connected.

U. staccato note – to be
    separated from other notes
    and shortened.

V. pick-up note – extra note
    at the beginning of a piece
    of music.

W. tied quarter notes – equal
    one half note.

X. dotted eighth note

Y. tenuto note – to be
    lengthened slightly.

Z. accented note – to be
    played louder than the
    surrounding notes.

After completing the test, turn to part 135.

Check your answers with those in the key that follows. Grade your results, thus:

25 to 30 correct answers: you have mastered the material. However, be sure to review the questions you missed before proceeding to Chapter 3.

24 or fewer correct answers: You seem to need a review. Read the chapter again before going on to Chapter 3.

answers and review index

3 / Notational Components of Melody

Music as we know it seldom consists of rhythm alone. It also includes MELODY, the subject of this chapter. You will recall that in the first chapter you learned to locate the highest and lowest notes in a passage of music. Now it is time to consider all the notes you see on a staff, how the staff is used as a framework for notating melody, and how the staff is related to a piano keyboard. A system of organizing notes, or tones, into scales based on a particular key tone will also be introduced.

At the conclusion of this chapter, you will be asked to demonstrate your knowledge of the music staff by:

1. Recognizing a definition of pitch.
2. Recalling the names of notes in the treble clef.
3. Recalling the names of notes in the bass clef.
4. Matching the symbols for sharps, flats, and naturals with their proper descriptions.
5. Identifying an octave on the staff.
6. Recognizing ledger lines.

Using a replica of the piano keyboard, you will be asked to do the following things:

1. Recall from memory the names of the notes of the white keys.
2. Demonstrate an understanding of the relationship between sharps and flats and the black keys on the piano keyboard.
3. Identify an octave on the piano keyboard.

You will be introduced to the concept of a major scale and will be required to do the following:

1. Identify whole steps and half steps.
2. Recognize the places in the major scale where half steps are located.
3. Recognize the definition of a key signature.
4. Identify a key signature.
5. Recognize the key signatures for the keys of C major, G major, and F major.

Turn to part 137.

The highness or lowness of a tone is called its PITCH. As you learned earlier, the pitch of a note is determined by its placement on the staff. The higher it is placed on the staff, the higher is its pitch; and the lower it is on the staff, the lower its pitch.

Notes can be placed on any line   or any space of the staff, depending on the pitch desired. Each of these lines and spaces has a letter name – A, B, C, D, E, F, or G. After the letter G   the pitches start over again with A. There is no such note as H.

Can you identify the notes of the treble clef on the staff below? If so, choose the alternative that properly identifies all of the notes from left to right.* Then turn to the part indicated.

alternatives   part

a. I'm not familiar with this aspect of music.
     Please explain it.   139

b. C G A E D   144

c. B G F E D   142

d. B F G D C   140

* If you have already answered the question once, correctly answer it again and continue the program as directed.

Use the Shield

These notes spell _____ .

BADGE

Here is a longer one. The word is _____ .

CABBAGE

These notes spell _____ .

DEED

These letters do not spell a word. The notes are ___, ___, ___,
___, ___ .

C, D, G, F, B

Now return to part 137.

The names of the notes in the treble clef are easy to learn once you understand the system for naming lines and spaces of the staff. We'll start with the note called MIDDLE C - found between the treble clef and the bass clef.

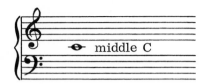

The middle-C line serves the same purpose as the other lines of the staff. The space above it is D, and the notes continue to rise on the staff in alphabetical order, thus: C, D, E, F, G. After G the musical alphabet starts over again with A (see the example below).

| C | D | E | F | G | A | B | C | D | E | F | G |

Notice that every line, and every space is given a note.

Use the Shield

This note, because it is between the treble and bass clefs, is called middle ___.

C

The note directly above middle C is ___.

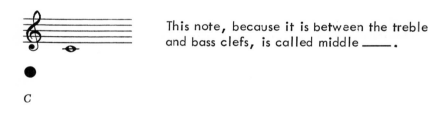

D

The fifth note up from middle C is called ___.

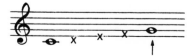

G

Go to part 141.

Right. Let's see if you can do as well with the next musical example.
Turn to part 146.

Use the Shield

After G   the letters start over again
with ____ .

●

A

This note is called ____ .

●

D

An easy way to remember the names of the spaces is to notice the
word they spell when read from bottom to top.

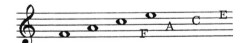

From bottom to top   the spaces spell the word _____ .

●

FACE

 Once you know the names of the spaces
you can figure out the names of the other
notes.
From left to right, these notes are ____ ,
____ , and ____ .

●

F, A, and G

Turn to part 143.

142

No, you started out right on B, but the other notes were incorrect. For an explanation, go to part 145.

---

143 *Use the Shield*

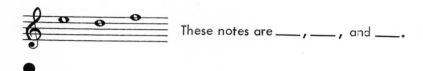

These notes are ____, ____, and ____.

●

E, D, F (E is the last space and, therefore, the last letter in the word FACE.)

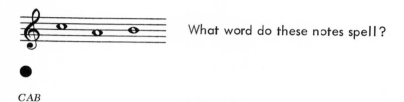

What word do these notes spell?

●

CAB

What word do these notes spell?

●

AGE

Do these two notes have the same name? What are their names?

●

Yes: They are both C, but the lower one is frequently called middle C.

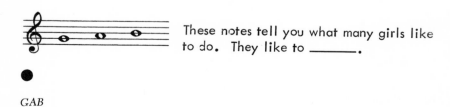

These notes tell you what many girls like to do. They like to _____.

●

GAB

Turn to part 138.

That wasn't quite right. Go on to part 145.

Take a close look at the notes on the staff below. The note on the first line below the staff is middle C.

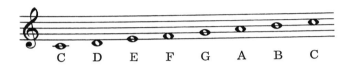

C D E F G A B C

After middle C the notes go up alphabetically, falling alternately on each line and each space, to G. They then start over again with A and continue as before. Here is a speedy way to remember the notes of the treble clef:

1. Learn middle C and the space above it (D).
2. Learn the names of the spaces, from the bottom to the top. (They spell the word FACE.)
3. If you need to identify a line, determine what the space directly below it is named, and then go up alphabetically.

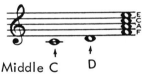

Middle C   D

If a short drill on the notes of the treble clef would help fix them in your mind, go to part 139.

If you are sure that you know the notes well enough, return to part 137.

146

What are the names of the notes on this staff?

alternatives   part

  a. I need to review this concept.   139

  b. E F A G F E D   148

  c. E G D C B A F   152

  d. G B F E D C A   150

Notes in the bass clef are alphabetical, just as those of the treble clef. They also go from A through G and then begin over with A. However, they must be learned separately because they fall on different lines and spaces of the staff.

The first two notes you need to learn are F and G.

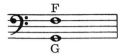

In the example observe the bass-clef sign, its two dots, and the staff line between the dots. THE LINE BETWEEN THE DOTS OF THE BASS-CLEF SIGN IS ALWAYS CALLED F. Thus, the note you see on that line is F.

The second note you need to remember is on the bottom line of the staff – the G line. Memorize these two notes, and from them you can figure out all other notes in the bass clef. For example, a note on the bottom space (right above G) would be A. (Remember, notes go from A to G and then start over with A.) All the names of notes in the bass clef are shown below.

Turn to part 151.

148

You seem to be confused and in need of an explanation of the notes of the treble clef. Go on to part 149.

149

The note on the first line below the staff is middle C.

After middle C the notes go up the staff alphabetically, falling alternately on lines and spaces. After G, the second line of the treble clef, the notes start over alphabetically with A and continue as before.

A speedy way to remember the notes of the treble clef is to use the following steps:

1. Learn middle C and the note (D) in the space directly above it.
2. Learn the names of the spaces, from the bottom to the top. They spell the word FACE.
3. When you need to identify a line, first determine the letter name of the space directly under it and then go up alphabetically.

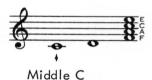

Middle C

If you would like a detailed exercise now, turn to part 139.

If you don't think you need the exercise, return to part 146.

You made a mistake and need an explanation to clarify the problem. Go to part 149.

Use the Shield

Probably the easiest note to learn in the bass clef is found on the line between the dots of the bass-clef sign. That note is ___.

●

F

Another important note in the bass clef is found on the bottom line. That note is___.

●

G

Counting one note for each line AND for each space above G, this note is found to be ___.

●

C

In both the treble and the bass clefs, notes are named A, B, C, D, E, F, G. The note after G is always ___.

●

A

This note is on the space directly under F. It is named ___.

●

E

These two important notes of the bass clef are ___ and ___.

●

F, G

Continue in part 153.

152

Right. You have again identified the notes in the treble clef correctly. Now go to part 154.

---

153   *Use the Shield*

From left to right, these notes spell a word. What is the word?

●

FAD

From left to right, what word do these notes spell?

●

AGE

Do these three notes spell a word?

●

Yes, BEG

These notes do not spell a word. What are their names?

●

A, F, G, and C

What long word do these notes spell?

●

BAGGAGE

If you feel the need for another review, reread the material that begins in part 147.

If not, return to part 154.

Although they use the same letters, the lines and spaces of the bass clef do not have the same names as those in the treble clef. In the example below are several notes in the bass clef. Can you identify the notes and select the corresponding alternative from those listed? *

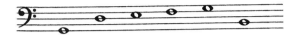

alternatives   part

   a. I don't know the notes of the bass clef.
      Where is an explanation?   147

   b. G B C D E G   160

   c. G D E F G B   156

   d. A C D E F B   158

  * If you have already answered the question once, correctly answer it again, and continue the program.

Now try this longer series of notes in the bass clef. Name the notes in the following example.

alternatives   part

   a. I could use a review.   147

   b. G E B C A G C   159

   c. G E B C A F C   161

   d. G E C B A G C   157

156

You are right. For your next question   go to part 155.

157

You should not be confused by the different stems on the notes. The place of the note on the staff determines the note name, and the stem helps to determine only the rhythm.

An explanation of the note names for the bass clef can be found in part 163.

You seem to have confused the notes. You will find the explanation you need in part 160.

Good. The next question will test your knowledge of some musical symbols that are used on the staff. Please turn to part 162.

160

Some of the notes you chose are right, but you did make a mistake.

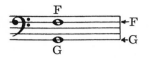 Two lines are particularly important for re-membering notes in the bass clef. Do you see the two dots in the bass-clef sign? Between them is the first important line. Notes on that line are always named F. The bottom line of the staff is always called G. From those two notes you can determine the other notes on the clef. For example, a note on the first space (right above G) would be A. As in the treble clef, the notes go from A to G and then start over with A.

Be sure to assign every line and every space a letter. By being careful not to skip notes, and by remembering the two key lines illustrated in the example at the top of the page, you can readily recall the notes of the bass clef.

If you would like to do a short exercise on the bass clef, turn to part 151.

If you feel that the exercise is not necessary, return to part 154.

161

You have made a mistake somewhere. Let's see if we can determine why. Go to part 163.

The column on the left shows some musical symbols. The center column lists their names in a different order. The right column states the purpose of each symbol, also in scrambled order. Determine which alternative matches the three columns properly (your answers will read something like A-1-W or B-3-X).

Symbol	Name	Meaning
A. ♭	1. ledger lines	W. lines above and below the regular staff
B. ♯	2. natural	X. raises the pitch of a note by one-half step
C. ♮	3. sharp	Y. lowers the pitch of a note by one-half step
D. ▤	4. flat	Z. cancels the effect of previous sharps or flats

alternatives

part

a. I'm not sure. Please show me.   164

b. A-2-Y
   B-3-Z
   C-4-X
   D-1-W   168

c. A-4-Y
   B-3-X
   C-2-Z
   D-1-W   170

d. A-4-Y
   B-2-Z
   C-3-X
   D-1-W   165

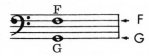

F ← F The two notes on the staff at the left are im-

G ← G portant ones for you to memorize immediately.

Notice the two dots in the bass clef sign and the line between. Notes on that line are always named F.

The other important note – on the bottom line of the staff – is always called G. By remembering the names ot these two notes, you can determine the other notes in the bass clef. For example, a note on the space right above G would be A. (Remember, notes go from A to G and then start over with A.)

G   A   B   C   D   E   F   G   A

Be sure to assign a note to every line and every space. By being careful not to skip a line or a space and by remembering the two key notes in the example at the top of the page, you will find it easy to recall the notes of the bass clef.

If you would like to do a short exercise on the bass clef, turn to part 151.

If not, return to the question in part 155.

You are to be congratulated for resisting the impulse to guess. Earlier in this chapter we talked about notes and how they follow the alphabet as they go up or down the staff. We learned that as the pitch rises the notes go through the alphabet from A to G and then start over.

Let's pretend for a moment that the distance between the notes A and B could be measured as one half inch, thus:

What kind of symbol would you use if you wanted to indicate a note half way between them? Well, you have a choice. You can use a SHARP (♯) with the bottom note, A. THE SHARP RAISES THE PITCH OF A NOTE BY ONE HALF STEP. The new note, called A sharp, would be half way between A and B.

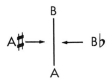

The other choice you have is to use a FLAT (♭) with the top note, B. THE FLAT LOWERS THE PITCH OF THE NOTE BY ONE HALF STEP. The new note would be called B flat. B flat is the same note as A sharp, in that the sound of the two is the same; but they appear to be different on the staff.

Continue in part 166.

165

No, you must have mixed up the answers somewhere. A one-page review should help you find your error. Turn to part 169.

Turn to part 169.

166

To review then, this is a sharp: ♯. It raises the pitch of a note by one half step. This is a flat: ♭. It lowers the pitch of a note by one half step. The next musical symbol you saw was a natural: ♮. A NATURAL CANCELS THE EFFECT OF PREVIOUS SHARPS OR FLATS. For example, if you wanted to write three notes in a row, C, then C sharp, and C again, you would put a natural by the last C to tell the performer to cancel the effect of the previous sharp. (See the example.)

The first note and the third note are the same. The natural sign would not be necessary if the middle note were removed.

In Chapter I you learned about staff lines. When you want to write a note that goes higher (or lower) than the staff, you will use short lines called LEDGER LINES to put the note on. Recall the use of a ledger line earlier in this chapter for the notation of middle C.

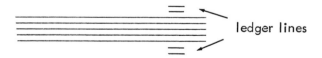

ledger lines

Now return to the question in part 162.

You were asked to identify an octave. Recall that the notes of the staff are named from A through G, and then they start over again with A. The distance from one A through the next A is called an octave. B through B, C through C, D through D, and so forth, are also octaves.

Which measure has the octave in this example?

In measure 1 the bottom note is D. It is one step above middle C (see part 145 if you have forgotten how to figure out the notes). Counting up one note for each line and each space, the top note in measure 1 is C. D to C is not an octave.

In measure number 2 the bottom note is still D, but the top note is one step higher than before. The top note in measure 2 is D. From D to D is an octave, so measure 2 is the answer.

Now return to the question in part 171.

168

The answer you chose indicates you should review these symbols. Go on to part 169.

169

A SHARP (♯) RAISES A NOTE ONE HALF STEP. For example, note number 1 below is A, and note number 2 is A sharp. A sharp is one half step above A, and, thus, is half way between A and B.

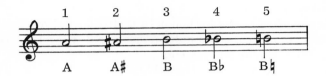

A FLAT (♭) LOWERS A NOTE BY ONE HALF STEP. Note number 3 is B. Number 4 is B-flat. B-flat is one half step below B, and is half way between A and B. In other words, B-flat and A-sharp have the same sound, but appear to be different on the printed page.

THE NATURAL (♮) CANCELS THE EFFECT OF ANY PREVIOUS SHARPS OR FLATS. Note number 5 needs a natural to tell you not to continue playing the flat which was placed before note number 4.

If a note is too high (or too low) to be written on the five-line staff, we can extend the staff by adding short lines where needed. These short lines are called LEDGER LINES.

Now return to the question in part 162 .

Very good!

1. The sharp (♯) raises a note by one half step.

2. The flat (♭) lowers a note by one half step.

3. The natural (♮) cancels the effect of previous sharps and flats.

4. Ledger lines are used when the pitch is so high or so low that the note must be written above or below the staff.

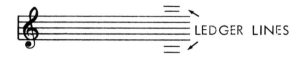

LEDGER LINES

Now go to part 171.

Another term you should know is OCTAVE. Which of the measures below (1, 2, or 3) is an example of an octave?

alternatives	part
a. I don't know.	167
b. measure 1	174
c. measure 2	172
d. measure 3	176

172

No, it seems you need an explanation. Go on to part 173.

173

You were asked to identify an octave. When learning the notes of the staff, you learned that the notes go from A through G and then start over again with A. The distance from A to A is called an octave. B to B, C to C, D to D, etc., are also octaves.

Let's look at an example:

In measure number 1 the bottom note is D. It is one step above middle C (see part 145 if you don't remember how to figure out the notes). Count up one note for each line and each space; the top note in measure 1 is C. From D to C is not an octave.

In measure 2 the bottom note is still D but the top note is one step higher than in measure 1. The top note in measure 2 is D. From D to D is an octave, so measure 2 is the answer.

Return to part 171.

Right! An octave is the distance from A to A, B to B, C to C, D to D, and so on. Measure 1 was from E to E.

Until now we have been dealing with music as it is written on the staff. Obviously music must be played or sung to be heard. The most common musical instrument is the human voice. Perhaps the next most widely used instrument is the piano. With your present knowledge of music it is time to acquaint yourself with the piano keyboard. To do this go to part 178.

While learning the names of notes from A to G, you also learned the position of middle C on the staff - between the bass and treble clefs.

The first note to learn on the piano is also middle C. You might wonder how many notes are named C on the keyboard. There are quite a few - one for every octave.

In the picture of the keyboard below, you will note that the black keys are arranged in groups of two or three. These groups are repeated up and down the keyboard.

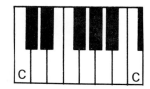

The first thing you need to remember is that the notes A, B, C, D, E, F, G are the long, white keys. The black keys are for sharps or flats.

Directly to the LEFT of the two black keys is C. Find C on the picture of the keyboard. Between the two black keys and right next to C, is D. Then come E, F, G, A, and B (all white keys). Then the notes start over with C again.

For the present you should fix in your mind two particular white keys: the C directly left of the two black keys, and the F directly left of the three black keys. Find F on the keyboard.

Turn to part 177.

176

No, not quite. To understand why, go to part 173.

177

Use the Shield

On the piano keyboard the sharps and flats are generally found on the keys colored _____.

●

black

The notes A, B, C, D, E, F, and G are on the _____colored keys.

●

white

The black keys are in groups of two and three. Directly left of the group of two black keys is the note ____ .

●

C

This arrow is pointing to the note ____ .

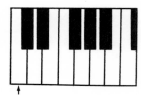

●

C

The arrow in the above frame is pointing to the key just (<u>left / right</u>) of the two black keys.

●

left

Does C appear on the keyboard more than one time?

●

yes

Continue in part 182.

A section of the piano keyboard is pictured below. Notice that the short black keys are in alternating groups of two and three.

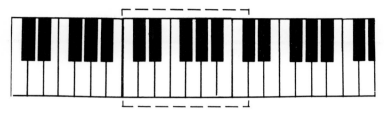

When a picture of the keyboard is used hereafter, only a small section – like the one within the dotted lines – will be shown.

Obviously every key on the piano will sound a note, and that note can be written on the staff. The notes on the piano keyboard have the same names as notes on the staff (A, B, C, D, E, F, G, A, B, etc.), and you should learn them.

In the section of the keyboard pictured below, five of the keys are numbered. Can you select the correct alternative by identifying the letter name of each numbered key? *

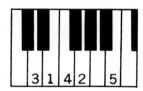

alternatives	part
a. I am not familiar with the piano keyboard. Will you explain it to me?	175
b. 1 = B 2 = A 3 = D 4 = C 5 = F	185
c. 1 = E 2 = F 3 = G 4 = A 5 = D	181
d. 1 = E 2 = G 3 = D 4 = F 5 = B	179

* If you have already answered this question once, correctly answer it again and continue the program.

179

Excellent. Here's hoping you can do as well on the next question, which is similar. Go to part 180.

180

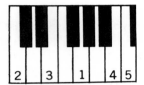

Choose the alternative which properly identifies all five of the keys numbered above.

alternatives

		page
a.	I am uncertain about this question.	175
b.	1 = G 2 = C 3 = E 4 = B 5 = C	189
c.	1 = D 2 = F 3 = B 4 = F 5 = G	187
d.	1 = G 2 = F 3 = E 4 = B 5 = C	183

No, that wasn't entirely correct. For an explanation of this question, go to part 186.

Use the Shield

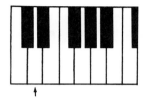

The white note directly above C is ___ .

●

D

The key to the left of the three black notes is the note ___ .

●

F

In this picture, number 1 is the note ___ , and number 2 is the note ___ .

●

C, F

Here, number 1 is the note ___ , and number 2 is the note ___ .

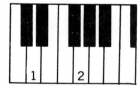

●

D, G

By remembering C and F, you can find all the other notes. Which of the two numbered notes is F?

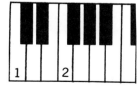

●

number 2

Continue in part 184.

183

You missed one note and should review the subject. There's a brief review for you in part 188.

---

184 *Use the Shield*

What are the names of notes 1, 2, and 3 here?

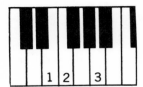

●

E, F, A

What are the names of the next three that are numbered?

●

D, E, A

Of the notes numbered, which is A?

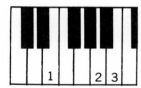

●

2

Which key in that last frame is E?

●

1

What key is number 3 in the example above?

●

B

In this example which note is G?

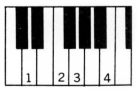

●

3

In the above example, what notes are 2 and 4?

●

F, B

Now return to the question in part 178.

You were mistaken in your identification of piano keys. Read on to part 186.

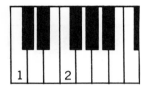

There are two keys that can serve as guideposts for all keys. The first one is directly left of the two black keys (number 1 in the example above). That key is C. The second guidepost is F; it is directly left of the three black keys (number 2).

Remember also that all the white keys are used for the notes A, B, C, D, E, F, and G. The black keys are used for sharps and flats.

By recalling the positions of C and F on the keyboard, you can determine all the other notes. STUDY THE ABOVE EXAMPLE AND LEARN TO IDENTIFY THE POSITION OF EACH NOTE BEFORE GOING ON.

The preceding discussion is intended only as a short reminder. If you have not had previous experience with the piano keyboard or if you feel insecure about the note names, turn to part 177.

If you think the reminder has been sufficient, return to the question in part 178.

187

That alternative was incorrect. See if the discussion below will refresh your memory. Go to part 188.

188

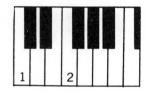

There are two keys you need to recognize quickly when you look at a keyboard. The first is directly left of the two black keys (number 1). It is C. The second key is F, which is directly left of the three black keys (number 2).

Remember also that the notes A, B, C, D, E, F, and G are the white keys. The black keys are used for sharps and flats.

By remembering the places of C and F on the keyboard, you can determine all the other notes. STUDY THE ABOVE EXAMPLE BEFORE GOING ON.

The above discussion is intended only as a short reminder. If you have not had previous experience with the piano keyboard, or if you feel that you need a longer review, turn to part 177.

If you are sure the above discussion is a sufficient reminder, return to the question in part 180.

You chose the proper alternative. Are you ready to go to something else? (The appropriate response is "yes.") Fine, go to part 190.

Not only do the white keys of the piano have names, but the black keys have names as well. Identify the black keys in the following example to pick your alternative.

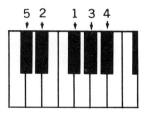

alternatives   part

    a. I think I should let you show me.   191

    b. 1 = G flat or F sharp
        2 = D flat or C sharp
        3 = A flat or G sharp
        4 = B sharp or C flat
        5 = C sharp or D flat   195

    c. 1 = F sharp or G flat
        2 = D sharp or E flat
        3 = A flat or G sharp
        4 = A sharp or B flat
        5 = D flat or C sharp   192

    d. 1 = F sharp or G flat
        2 = E flat or D sharp
        3 = A sharp or B flat
        4 = B sharp or C flat
        5 = C sharp or D flat   197

191

The first thing to remember about black keys is that they are used only as sharps and flats. The next thing you need to understand is that a black key can have two names.

The black key in the example on the right is between F and G. It can be called F sharp because it is directly above F; or it can be called G flat because it is directly below G. Both names (F sharp and G flat) are correct, and they refer to the same note. Let's look at another example:

Arrow 1 points out a black key that is half way between D and E. Therefore the key can be called D sharp or E flat. Either name is correct, depending upon the music in which the note is used.

The black key under arrow 2 is between G and A. It can therefore be called G sharp or A flat. The third arrow is pointing out the black key between A and B, which can be called A sharp or B flat. Thus, every black key has two possible names.

Use the Shield

This black key between C and D can be called C sharp or _____. Either name is correct.

●

D flat

This black key between F and G can, therefore, be called either _____ sharp or _____ flat.

●

F sharp, G flat

The two names of this black key are ___ and ___ .

●

A sharp, B flat

Continue in part 193.

That was a good choice. Obviously you realize that a black key be-tween two white keys has two names.

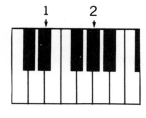

The black key on the left can properly be called either C sharp – because it is directly above C – or D flat – be-cause it is directly below D.

Now we must return to the word "octave," which you learned earlier.*

The next step in the program is in part 196.

*See part 167 if you would like to refresh your memory about an octave.

Use the Shield

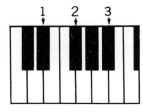

Black key number 1 can be called ____ or ____ .

●

D sharp, E flat

Black key number 2 (in the above example) is ____ or ____ .

●

G sharp, A flat

Which arrow is pointing to A sharp?

●

arrow 3

Which arrow is pointing to F sharp? (above)

●

arrow 2

Continue in part 194.

194

Use the Shield

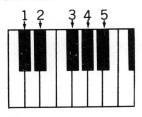

Which arrow is pointing to D flat?

●

arrow 1

Another name for the key we call D flat is _____ .

●

C sharp

C sharp and D flat are the two names for the key under arrow number _____ .

●

one

The two names for the key under arrow 3 are _____ and _____ .

●

F sharp, G flat

A-sharp, or B flat, is found under arrow number _____ .

●

five

Arrow number 4 points at G sharp or _____ .

●

A flat

Arrow number 2 points at _____ or _____ .

●

D sharp, E flat

Now carefully choose the correct answer to the question in part 190.

The black keys are causing you some confusion. Read carefully the brief explanation in part 198.

At the base of the keyboard below are three numbered arrows. One of them covers exactly an octave on the keyboard. The other two do not. Which arrow points out an octave?

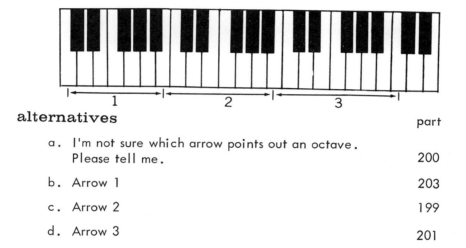

alternatives   part

   a. I'm not sure which arrow points out an octave.
       Please tell me.   200

   b. Arrow 1   203

   c. Arrow 2   199

   d. Arrow 3   201

197

No, your alternative mixed some of the notes. Go on to part 198.

198

Here are four points for you to remember:

1. The black keys are used for sharps and flats only.

2. Every black key has two names, one using a sharp (♯), and the other using a flat (♭).

3. Every black key is between two white keys.
   For example, this one is between C and D:

4. The black key is named by putting a sharp with the name of the lower white key (here, C sharp) or by putting a flat with the name of the higher white key (here, D flat). Both C sharp and D flat are correct names for this black key.

The same is true with any black key. If you find the names of the two white keys on either side, and PUT A SHARP WITH THE LOWER ONE, OR A FLAT WITH THE HIGHER ONE, you will have the black-key name.

This was only a short review. If the concept of black keys still seems at all strange to you, turn to part 191.

If this review is sufficient, return to the question in part 190.

That is correct. An octave is the distance from A to A, B to B, C to C, and so forth, whether on the staff or on a keyboard. For your next step go to part 204.

When we first used the term OCTAVE we were talking about the music staff. If you start with A on the staff and proceed through G, you must continue to A to complete the octave. IT IS EXACTLY THE SAME ON THE PIANO KEYBOARD. An octave is the distance from A to A, B to B, C to C, and so forth, whether on the staff or on the keyboard.

When asked to find an octave on the keyboard, you need to first name the starting key; then count up the music alphabet (starting over after G) until you arrive at the same letter name you started with. In doing so you will cover an octave.

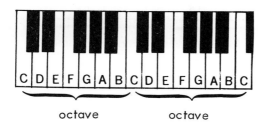

octave   octave

Two octaves are marked in the above example (C to C to C). There are many other octaves shown as well: D to D, F to F, A to A, etc.

Briefly, to find an octave on the keyboard, identify any key and find the nearest key with the same letter name. An octave is located between the two closest keys of the same name.

Now you should find it easy to identify the octave in part 196.

201

Well, you've made an error. You should read the next part about keyboard octaves. Go on to part 202.

---

202   When we first used the term OCTAVE, we were talking about the music staff. Notes on the staff go from A through G, and then continue with A to complete an octave. IT IS EXACTLY THE SAME ON THE PIANO KEYBOARD. An octave goes from A to A, B to B, C to C, and so on, whether on the staff or on the keyboard.

When you are asked to find an octave on the keyboard, you need first the name of the starting key. Then count up the alphabet (after G, start again with A) on the keyboard until you arrive at the same letter name again. That distance is an octave.

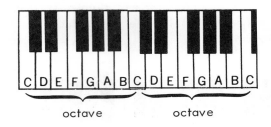

Two octaves are marked on the keyboard above(C to C to C). If you examine the keyboard you will see that there are many other octaves as well: D to D, F to F, A to A, and so on.

In summary, all that is needed to locate an octave on the keyboard is to find the nearest key to any given key with the same letter name. The distance covered is an octave.

Return to the original question now and identify the octave in part 196.

No, that was too small for an octave.   To learn why, turn to part 202.

In the next example, the brackets show the two locations on the keyboard where there are no black keys between the white keys.

If there is NO black key between two white keys, the white keys are
said to be:

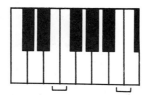

alternatives   part

    a.   one half step apart   207

    b.   one whole step apart   205

205

The mistake on your answer is easy to correct. Please read part 206.

206

If you start at the left of the keyboard and play every note (that is, every white and black key) from left to right, you are playing HALF STEPS. A half step is the smallest step on the piano keyboard. EVERY NOTE IS ONE HALF STEP FROM ITS CLOSEST NEIGHBOR.

If any two keys, regardless of their colors, do not have another key between them, the two keys are a half step apart. (See the example.)

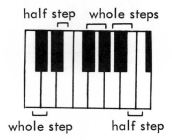

Notice, however, that if there is a key between the two given keys, they are a whole step apart. (See the example.)

Return to the question in part 204.

Right. If there is no black key between two white keys, the white keys are one half step apart. Likewise, if there is a black key between them, the white keys are a whole step apart. Now go to part 208.

Which white keys in this next example are only one half step from each other?

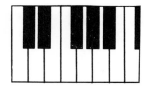

alternatives

	part
a. I believe you should explain it.	212
b. E to F	209
c. E to F and B to C	213
d. C to D and F to G	211

209

Your answer was partially right but you need a brief explanation. You will find it in part 210.

210

You were asked to show which white keys are only one half step apart. Earlier, you learned that each key on the piano keyboard is one half step from its nearest neighboring key, black or white.

C sharp

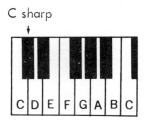

Look at the note C in the example. The nearest key to the right of C is the black key C sharp directly to its right. That distance is one half step. From the black key C sharp to its nearest neighbor on the right (D) is also one half step. Thus, from C to D is two half steps, or one whole step.

We may generalize the following: If there is a key between any two other keys, the two keys are one WHOLE step apart. If there is no key between them, the keys are a HALF step apart.

Therefore, when you are asked to show which white keys are only one half step apart, the white keys WITHOUT BLACK KEYS BETWEEN THEM are the ones you must find.

With that in mind, try again to answer the question in part 208.

You've overlooked an important point. To discover it go to part 210.

The problem is to find which white keys on a piano keyboard are only one half step apart. Do you recall the statement made earlier that every key is only one half step from its nearest neighboring key, black or white?

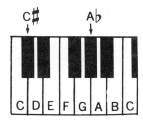

Look at the note C in the example. The nearest key to the right of C is the black key C sharp. Therefore, the distance from C to C sharp is one half step. From the black key C sharp to its nearest neighbor (D) is also one half step. Thus, there are two half steps from C to D – or one whole step.

We can conclude the following: If there is one key between any two keys, the two keys are one WHOLE step apart. If there is no key between them, the keys are one half step apart. For example, from C to D is a whole step because there is a black key between them. G to A flat is a half step because there is no note between them.

When you are asked to show which white keys are only one half step apart, the white keys WITHOUT BLACK KEYS BETWEEN THEM are the ones you must find. Keep that in mind as you complete the following sentences.

Continue in part 214.

213

Congratulations. You remembered that the distance from one key to its nearest neighbor is a half step. Therefore, the half steps are between E and F, and B and C. By learning the location of half steps, you have mastered one of the prime factors governing major scales. For more on this go to part 215.

---

214 *Use the Shield*

On the piano keyboard the distance from C to D is a _____ step.

●

whole (There is a black key between them.)

From B to C is a _____ step.

●

half (no key between)

From G to A flat is a _____ step.

●

half

From F sharp to G sharp is a _____ step.

●

whole (The key G is between.)

From E to F sharp is a _____ step.

●

whole (F is between.)

Now return to the question in part 208.

C-major scale

half steps

A scale is a series of notes within any octave (e.g., C to C or D to D) that follows a particular arrangement of whole and half steps. The effect of the arrangement is to give one tone dominance over the others so that they seem to be "pulled" toward it. If you count the first note in the octave as number 1 and give the rest of the notes, in order of ascending pitch, the numbers 2 to 8, major scales will have half steps between steps 3 and 4 and 7 and 8 (see the example above). All other steps are whole steps.

To summarize, a major scale consists of eight notes within an octave arranged in a set pattern of whole steps and half steps. The half steps lie between steps 3 to 4 and 7 to 8.

Let's see if you can apply this rule to another major scale. In the key of G major (beginning and ending on G), the half steps will fall between which notes?

G-major scale

alternatives

		page
a.	I'm not too sure. Please explain further.	217
b.	B sharp to C and F sharp to G	221
c.	E to F and B to C	218
d.	B to C and F sharp to G	216

216

Correct. The half steps must fall between steps 3 and 4 and 7 and 8 of the major scale. In the key of G major (GABCDEF♯G), the half steps must fall between B and C and F and G. Because F to G is a whole step (there is a black key between them), the step must be made smaller. This is done by raising the F to F sharp. The resulting step (F sharp to G) is the desired half step. The key of G major will therefore always have F sharp in it. Try applying the major-scale pattern to another key - in part 223.

217

All right, let's take a more detailed look at the major scale.

C-major scale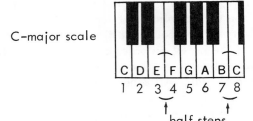

Look closely at the octave from C to C in the example. The keys are numbered 1 through 8 from one C to the next, left to right. As you can see, there is no black key between E and F (steps 3 and 4). Neither is there a black key between B and C (steps 7 and 8). BECAUSE THERE ARE NO KEYS BETWEEN THESE NOTES THEY ARE ONLY ONE HALF STEP APART.

We are using the C-major scale to observe where the half steps fall in a major scale, because it shows the half steps without using black keys. All other major scales use some black keys to get the half steps in the right places. Remember: ALL MAJOR SCALES HAVE HALF STEPS BETWEEN NOTES 3 AND 4 AND 7 AND 8 OF THE ASCENDING SCALE.

You can form a major scale in any octave by numbering the notes 1 through 8, as we did above, and putting half steps in the designated places, making sure all other steps are whole steps. For example:

F-major scale:

B♭ is needed here for the half step from 3 to 4.

Go to part 219.

Not quite. You forgot one important detail, a sharp on the F. To brush up on this turn to part 222.

Here is another example:

A-major scale: A B C♯ D E F♯ G♯ A
                  1 2 3 ‿4 5 6   7‿ 8
                        ↑   ↑   ↑
                  Sharps are needed here to conform
                  to the major-scale pattern of whole
                  steps and half steps.

Use the Shield

If a major scale starts on G in the octave shown above, it will also end on _____ .

●

G

If you number the notes in the scale, G will be note number 1 and B will be note number _____ .

●

3

Turn to part 220.

220

When numbering an octave for a major scale, you number the notes from 1 to _____ .

●

8

Every step in the major scale is a whole step except the steps 3–4 and _____ .

●

7 – 8

The steps 3–4 and 7–8 are (<u>whole</u> / half) steps.

●

half

Steps 3 and 4 in the G major scale fall on notes _____ and _____ .

●

B, C

Steps 7 and 8 fall on notes _____ and _____ in G major.

●

F♯, G

In a G-major scale, there are no keys between B and C, or between _____ and _____ .

●

F♯, G

Now return to part 215.

Did you misunderstand the question? In any event you need to give some more thought to the formation of a major scale. Go to part 222.

C-major scale

half steps

Look at the octave from C to C. We have given the keys the numbers 1 through 8, beginning and ending on C. As you can see, there is no black key between E and F (step 3 to 4). Neither is there a black key between B and C (step 7 to 8). Because there is no key between these notes, they are only one half step apart.

The C-major scale is used here to show the half steps of a major scale because the half steps fall naturally on the white keys of the piano. No black keys are needed for the scale of C major. All other major scales need to use some black keys for the half steps to fall in the right places. Remember: All major scales have half steps between notes 3 and 4 and 7 and 8.

You can form a major scale in any octave by numbering the notes 1 through 8 and putting half steps in the designated places. All other steps must be whole steps. For example:

A-major scale   A   B   C♯ D   E   F♯   G♯ A
                    1   2   3   4   5   6   7   8
                              half steps

F-major scale   F   G   A   B♭ C   D   E   F
                    1   2   3   4   5   6   7   8
                              half steps

Now return to the question in part 215.

223

Now see if you can find steps 3 to 4 and 7 to 8 in the key of F major.

F—major scale

When you have found them, choose the alternative below that correctly lists these steps as half steps:

alternatives

		part
a.	I'm still unsure.	226
b.	A to B flat and E to F	227
c.	B to C and E to F	229
d.	B flat to C and F sharp to G	225

Rather than continually writing and rewriting the sharps or flats before the notes that require them in a particular key, musicians long ago devised a system of grouping the sharps and flats next to the meter signature. Such a group is called the KEY SIGNATURE. Three key signatures are shown below.

 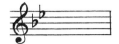 

A key signature may be defined as a group of sharps or flats appearing at the beginning of each staff of music to indicate the key of the music. Key signatures show the performer what notes in the scale must be altered in such a way that all steps of the scale are whole steps except steps 3 to 4 and 7 to 8, which are half steps. Thus, they establish the key of the music – just as a meter signature establishes the beat. Match the three examples on the left with the proper key on the right.

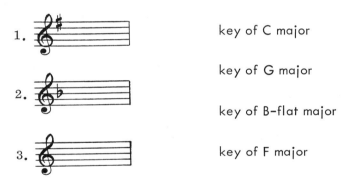

1.

key of C major

key of G major

2.

key of B-flat major

3.

key of F major

alternatives

part

a. I need an explanation before attempting to answer this question.

228

b. 1 = key of G major
2 = key of F major
3 = key of C major

235

c. 1 = key of F major
2 = key of B-flat major
3 = key of C major

233

d. 1 = key of C major
2 = key of F major
3 = key of G major

231

225

You have chosen the wrong alternative. Please read the explanation in part 230.

226

All right, let's examine the key of F major   step by step.

F major

First, number the notes from 1 to 8, beginning with the first note of the scale. For F major, begin on F – just as for G major, you begin on G. Note number 8, the last one, should have the same letter name as number 1.

F G A B C D E F
1 2 3 4 5 6 7 8

Since you are looking for steps 3 to 4 and 7 to 8, you now look for the notes which have the appropriate numbers. Steps 3 and 4 are A and B; 7 and 8 are E and F.

The next step is to make sure that steps 3 to 4 and 7 to 8 are half steps – that there are no keys between them. Since step 3 to 4 is A to B, there is a black key between them. An adjustment is needed. If you substitute B flat for B, the step becomes a half step and the problem is solved. F major will therefore always use B flat instead of B. Step 7 to 8 is E to F – a half step as it stands – so, no adjustment is needed there.

Return now to answer the question in part 223.

You are right. The half steps in the key of F major fall between A and B flat, and E and F. The key of F major will therefore always have a B flat.

As you have seen, certain keys always need to use flats or sharps to conform to the half-step spacing between steps 3 and 4 and 7 and 8 of their scales. Do you know how these sharps and flats are indicated on a music score? More on this subject in part 224.

Here is the explanation:

Earlier you learned that the key of G major would always need an F sharp to provide the half step between 7 and 8. The key signature for G major, therefore, is F sharp, as shown on the right.

We determined that F major would always need a B flat (part 226) to properly locate the half step between 3 and 4. F major will, therefore, always use B flat for its key signature.

Go to part 232.

229

No, you have chosen the wrong answer. Please read part 230.

230

F—major scale

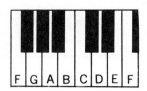

First you must number the notes from 1 through 8, beginning with the first note of the scale. (For F major, 1 will be F; for G major, G will be 1; and for A major, A, etc.) Number 8, the last note, should have the same letter name as the first one, thus:

```
F   G   A   B   C   D   E   F
1   2   3   4   5   6   7   8
```

You were asked to find steps 3 to 4 and 7 to 8, and these are now obvious. Steps 3 and 4 are A and B; 7 and 8 are E and F.

Next you must make sure that the steps from 3 to 4 and 7 to 8 are half steps – that is, that there are no black keys between them. In F major, step 3 to 4 is A to B, and there is a black key between them; it is not correct if left unadjusted. By substituting B flat for B, you can make it a half step and the problem is solved. F major will therefore always use B flat instead of B. Step 7 to 8 is E to F, a half step as it stands, and no adjustment is needed.

Return to part 223.

That alternative was incorrect. A brief review should clear up your problem. Go to part 234.

In the first scale studied, C major, we saw that the half steps are properly located without adding any sharps or flats (part 217). The C-major key signature, therefore, is indicated by the absence of sharps or flats.

Memorize these three key signatures; it will take but a minute:

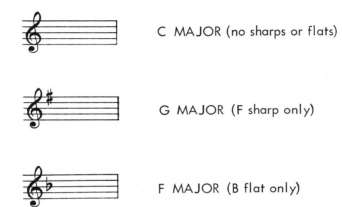

C MAJOR (no sharps or flats)

G MAJOR (F sharp only)

F MAJOR (B flat only)

Return to part 224.

233

You have mixed up two of the key signatures.   Go on to part 234.

234

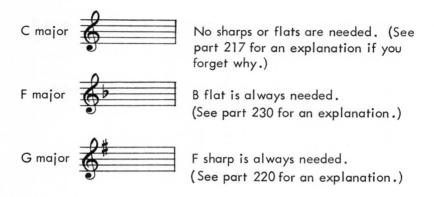

C major — No sharps or flats are needed. (See part 217 for an explanation if you forget why.)

F major — B flat is always needed. (See part 230 for an explanation.)

G major — F sharp is always needed. (See part 220 for an explanation.)

You should memorize these three key signatures before proceeding. They will be required of you later in the program.

Return to part 224 if you don't need the review in part 228.

Congratulations! You have now reached the end of Chapter 3 of the program. Although you don't need to memorize this list, you should take a careful look at each of the following key signatures.

 Key of D major: F sharp, C sharp

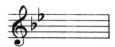 Key of B-flat major: B flat, E flat

 Key of A major: F sharp, C sharp, G sharp

 Key of E-flat major: B flat, E flat, A flat

 Key of E major: F sharp, C sharp, G sharp, D sharp

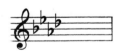 Key of A-flat major: B flat, E flat, A flat, D flat

You are now ready to take the Self-Evaluation Test, which begins in part 236.

Self-Evaluation Test

Match the musical terms and symbols on the left side of the page with their proper definitions from the list on the right.

_____ 1. pitch

       A. a group of sharps or flats placed at the beginning of the staff to identify the key.

_____ 2. octave

       B. raises the pitch of a note by one half step.

_____ 3. key signature

       C. comprised of whole steps except for steps 3 to 4 and 7 to 8, which are half steps.

_____ 4. sharp

       D. the distance from A to A, B to B, etc.

_____ 5. flat

       E. cancels previous sharps or flats.

_____ 6. natural

       F. the highness or lowness of a note.

_____ 7. major scale

       G. lowers the pitch of a note by one half step.

Select the best description from those on the right for each staff on the left and write your choice by the appropriate number.

_____ 8.

       H. ledger lines

_____ 9.

       I. key signature for G major

_____ 10.

       J. key signature for F major

_____ 11.

       K. key signature for C major

Go on to part 237.

Each of the notes on the staves below has a number. There are six notes in the treble clef and six in the bass clef. Name each note in the blank provided.

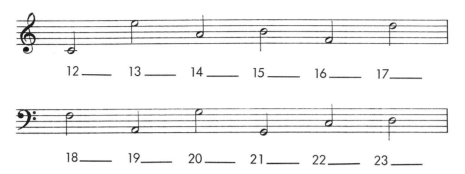

12 ____ 13 ____ 14 ____ 15 ____ 16 ____ 17 ____

18 ____ 19 ____ 20 ____ 21 ____ 22 ____ 23 ____

Identify each numbered key in the examples below by writing its name in the appropriate blank.

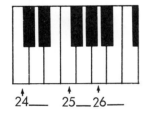 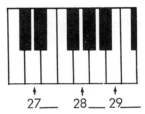

24 ____ 25 ____ 26 ____   27 ____ 28 ____ 29 ____

Match the numbered black keys with the appropriate letters from the right.

30 ____ 31 ____ 32 ____

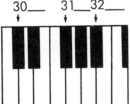

L.   F sharp or G flat

M.   C sharp or D flat

N.   A sharp or B flat

Using 1/1 for whole and 1/2 for half, write the fraction that properly describes the intervals shown on this keyboard.

34 ____

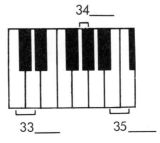

33 ____   35 ____

After completing the test, turn to part 238.

Check your answers with those in the key that follows. Grade your results thus:

28 to 35 correct answers: you have mastered the material. Review the questions you missed in the review index accompanying the key IMMEDIATE-LY. Then proceed to Chapter 4.

27 or fewer correct answers: you need to review the chapter before going on to Chapter 4.

answers and review index

1. F (pitch defined) 137
2. D (octave) 167
3. A (key signature defined) 224
4. B (sharps) 164
5. G (flats) 164
6. E (naturals) 166
7. C (major scale) 215
8. K (C-major key signature) 232
9. I (G-major key signature) 232
10. H (ledger lines) 166
11. J (F-major key signature) 232
12. C (notes of the treble clef) 139ff
13. E (notes of the treble clef) 139ff
14. A (notes of the treble clef) 139ff
15. B (notes of the treble clef) 139ff
16. F (notes of the treble clef) 139ff
17. D (notes of the treble clef) 139ff
18. F (notes of the bass clef) 147ff
19. A (notes of the bass clef) 147ff
20. G (notes of the bass clef) 147ff
21. G (notes of the bass clef) 147ff
22. C (notes of the bass clef) 147ff
23. D (notes of the bass clef) 147ff
24. C (piano keyboard, white keys) 175ff
25. F (piano keyboard, white keys) 175ff
26. A (piano keyboard, white keys) 175ff
27. D (piano keyboard, white keys) 175ff
28. G (piano keyboard, white keys) 175ff
29. B (piano keyboard, white keys) 175ff
30. M (piano keyboard, black keys) 191
31. L (piano keyboard, black keys) 191ff
32. N (piano keyboard, black keys) 191ff
33. 1/1 (piano keyboard intervals) 206
34. 1/2 (piano keyboard intervals) 206
35. 1/2 (piano keyboard intervals) 206

4 / Harmonic Structure of Music

In previous chapters, the basic aspects of rhythm and melody were presented. Let us now turn our attention to a third major component of music: harmony. In spite of the differences between pieces of music, close examination of tone combinations will reveal some common and often repeated patterns. In this chapter you will become acquainted with several such patterns. Now see what will be expected of you in this chapter.

objectives

1. Recall definitions for the terms harmony, chord, and interval.
2. Identify the basic intervals - the second, third, fourth, fifth, sixth, and seventh.
3. Recall the names of the major and minor intervals and of the perfect and imperfect intervals.
4. Identify major and minor thirds and sixths.
5. Identify perfect, augmented, and diminished fourths and fifths.
6. Recognize the definition of a triad and a statement of the differences between major and minor triads.
7. Determine whether a triad is major or minor.
8. Construct a triad on any given note.
9. Recognize which triads are primary (major) and which are secondary (minor) in any major key.
10. Recognize the I, IV, and V chords in the keys of D, B-flat, and E major.

Go on to part 240.

240

Professional musicians frequently find it difficult to agree on an all-inclusive definition of harmony because of its complexity. Basically though, harmony is the simultaneous sounding of two or more tones. The combination of notes that are sounded together is referred to as a chord. When persons sing together they are HARMONIZING, or making chords.

Which of the following statements IS concerned with harmony?

alternatives

part

a. The beat in that piece of music is
    really unusual.   242

b. Have you ever heard anyone who
    could sing so high?   244

c. They were out of tune at first, but
    now they sound good together.   248

Another term you need to recognize is INTERVAL. An interval is the difference in pitch between two tones that are played simultaneously. For example, the difference in pitch between C and D is smaller than the difference between C and E or C and F. Because the distance between the notes is different, their intervals are said to be different. In this example the interval between C and G is smaller than the interval between C and B:

From the alternatives below pick out both the smallest and the largest intervals.

alternatives

	smallest		largest		part
a.	1	and	4		246
b.	3	and	6		245
c.	3	and	4		243

242

No, that can't be right. Why? The statement you selected mentions the beat, or the pulse, of a musical selection. Beat and pulse have to do with the rhythm of music, not its harmony. Harmony is the sounding of two or more notes together, whether it involves two persons singing together or two instruments playing together. Now choose the correct response in part 240.

243

You are right about the smallest interval but wrong on the largest. Go to part 247.

No, that can't be right. A remark about a person's ability to sing high notes is a comment on the RANGE of his voice and has nothing to do with harmony. It takes two people or two instruments, singing or playing together, to make harmony. Now choose the correct response in part 240.

Correct. The farther apart notes are, the larger is the interval between them. Intervals are identified by numbers. The identifying number for each interval is the number of scale tones included therein.

For example, in the interval C to E there are three lines and spaces – C, D, and E – so the interval is called a THIRD. That information should help you answer your next question, in part 249.

third

246

Not quite right on either count. You should find out why in part 247.

247

An interval is the difference in pitch between two notes that are played

together. If you played the note D  and the note B

together, the B would be written directly above the D like this:

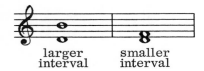

Those notes are farther apart than the notes D and F, if they were also

played together. Look at this comparison:

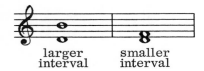

larger   smaller
interval   interval

Return to the question in part 241.

Of course. If persons are singing together (simultaneously but not in unison) they are singing harmony, even if it might be bad harmony. Turn to part 241.

Pick the alternative below that correctly identifies the intervals of a SECOND, FIFTH, and SIXTH in that order.

alternatives

part

a. I'm not sure. Where is the discussion on this point? 250

	second		fifth		sixth	
b.	4	and	7	and	1	253
c.	6	and	1	and	3	255
d.	6	and	2	and	1	257

While examining the problem, remember that an interval is the distance between two notes played together. Using the note D as a basis, here are some examples.

The bottom note is D, and the top note is E. The interval D to E encompasses only two lines and spaces and is, therefore, called a SECOND.

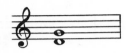

This interval has two notes: D and F. There is a line between them, namely E. This interval encompasses THREE lines and spaces, D, E, and F. It is a THIRD.

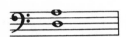

This interval encompasses D (the bottom note), E, F, and G (the top note). Because it encompasses four lines and spaces, it is a FOURTH.

This interval is in the bass clef. The bottom note is D. The interval encompasses D, E, F, G, and A; five lines and spaces. It is the interval of a FIFTH.

Using another example in the bass clef – this interval begins on A and goes up to F. It encompasses A, B, C, D, E, and F and is, therefore, a SIXTH.

By counting the bottom note and the top note of an interval plus all the lines and spaces between them, you can determine the size of the interval.

Use the Shield

What is the interval's size?

●

It encompasses C, D, E, and F—four lines and spaces. It is a fourth.

What is the size of this interval?

●

It encompasses seven lines and spaces: F, G, A, B, C, D, and E. It is a seventh.

Go to part 251.

Use the Shield

Identify this interval.

●

Since it covers only A and B, it is a second.

What is this interval? (Note the bass clef.)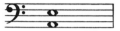

●

From the bottom note, A, the interval covers B, C, D, and E. It is therefore, a fifth.

Identify this last interval.

●

Covering all the lines and spaces between B and G (six of them), this interval is a sixth.

Return to answer the question in part 249.

Here we will be concerned with two kinds of intervals only: those that **252** are usually either major or minor and those that are usually either perfect, diminished, or augmented.

Do not guess on the next question. It is important that you fully understand this concept.

Which alternative correctly describes the intervals in the following example?

alternatives

part

a. I would prefer an explanation before
I select my response.   254

b. Intervals 1 and 4 are usually major or minor.
Intervals 2 and 3 are usually perfect,
diminished, or augmented.   261

c. Intervals 1 and 3 are usually major or minor.
Intervals 2 and 4 are usually perfect,
diminished, or augmented.   259

253

Not quite right. For an explanation, turn to part 256.

254

The example above includes a third, a fourth, a fifth, and a sixth. Two intervals are designated PERFECT – the fourths and fifths. By adding sharps or flats, you may augment or diminish perfect intervals. If a perfect interval is increased by one half step, it is said to be AUGMENTED. When it is made one half step smaller, it is termed DIMINISHED. Hence fourths and fifths may be perfect, augmented, or diminished.

Thirds and sixths are usually either major or minor (a minor sixth is one half step smaller than a major sixth). They cannot be referred to as perfect although they may, rarely, be augmented or diminished.

In summary, thirds and sixths are usually either major or minor. Fourths and fifths are perfect, augmented, or diminished.

QUESTION: Of the following intervals, which ones may be perfect? second, third, fourth, fifth, sixth, seventh.

ANSWER: Only fourths and fifths can be perfect.

Now answer the question in part 252.

No, that wasn't quite right. Let's examine the problem in part 256.

An interval is the distance between two notes played together. Here are some examples using the note D as a basis:

The bottom note is D and the top note is E. The interval D to E encompasses only two lines and spaces; it is therefore called a SECOND.

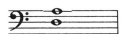
This interval has two notes: D and F. There is a line between them – E. This interval encompasses THREE lines and spaces, D, E, and F. It is a THIRD.

This interval encompasses D (the bottom note), E, F, and G (the top note). Because it encompasses four lines and spaces, it is a FOURTH.

This interval is in the bass clef, so the bottom note is D. The interval encompasses D, E, F, G, and A – five lines and spaces. It is the interval of a FIFTH.

This second interval in the bass clef begins on A and goes up to F. It encompasses A, B, C, D, E, and F and is therefore a SIXTH.

By counting the bottom note and the top note of an interval plus all the lines and spaces between them, you can determine the size of the interval.

Return and answer the question in part 249.

Right. Now that you have identified the basic interval sizes, let's examine the different kinds of intervals. Turn to part 252.

---

258   HOW TO DISTINGUISH BETWEEN MAJOR AND MINOR INTERVALS.

When first attempting to analyze intervals, it is probably necessary to use a piano keyboard. If no piano is available, use the facsimile of a keyboard on the back cover of the book. The following brief table shows that there is a difference of one tone between major and minor intervals:

	Tones		Tones
Major thirds	5	Major sixths	10
Minor thirds	4	Minor sixths	9

To prove this, find the note C on the keyboard. Now find the E directly above it. C to E (C, D, E) is a third. Is it major or minor? The table shows that a major third encompasses five tones. Counting the tones in this interval, we have: (1) C, a white key; (2) C♯, a black key; (3) D, a white key; (4) D♯, a black key; and (5) E, a white key.

There are five tones in the interval. It is a major third. Now, going to the note E again, find the C directly above it. From E to C is a sixth (E, F, G, A, B, C) but is it a major or a minor sixth? Count the tones in the intervals, thus: (1) E, white key; (2) F, white key; (3) F♯, black key; (4) G, white key; (5) G♯, black key; (6) A, white key; (7) A♯, black key; (8) B, white key; (9) C, white key.

Between E and C there are nine tones. Therefore the interval is a minor sixth. (See the table).

Go to part 260.

You must have overlooked something. For an explanation, turn to part 254.

IT IS NECESSARY TO COUNT ALL KEYS (BOTH BLACK AND WHITE) WHEN DETERMINING INTERVALS. Now its your turn to determine the nature of some intervals.

Use the Shield

Is this third major or minor?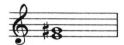

●

major; (It has five tones, E, F, F♯, G, and G♯.)

What is the name of this interval?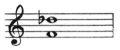

●

a sixth

Is it major or minor?

●

minor (There are nine tones: F, F♯, G, G♯, A, A♯, C, and C♯ (or D♭)

Is this sixth major or minor? (note the bass clef.)

●

minor (There are nine tones: C♯, D, D♯, E, F, F♯, G, G♯, A .)

Turn to part 262.

261

Very good. Thirds and sixths can be either major or minor. Fourths and fifths are perfect, diminished, or augmented.

Up to now we have been measuring intervals according to the lines and spaces they encompass on the staff. Musicians find this process laborious, and commit the intervals to memory instead. In the same way you know that 9 times 6 equals 54, the musician knows that the interval from D to G is a fourth. If sharps or flats are then added, it is easy to determine whether the interval is augmented or diminished. For more about measuring intervals go to part 263.

262

Use the Shield

What is this interval?

●

a third

Is it major or minor?

●

It has five tones, so it must be major. (A, A ♯ , B, C, and C ♯ .)

Major sixths encompass (how many) tones.

●

ten

Minor sixths contain _____ tones.

●

nine

Major thirds contain _____ tones.

●

five

Minor thirds contain _____ tones.

●

four

Now answer the question in part 263.

Because you have not yet acquired the musician's facility in recognizing intervals, we will measure intervals by the number of TONES they encompass. For example, the interval F to A contains five tones: F, F♯, G, G♯, and A.

1. Thirds containing five tones are major thirds.
2. Thirds containing four tones are minor thirds.
3. Sixths containing ten tones are major sixths.
4. Sixths containing nine tones are minor sixths.

In answering the next question and others that follow, you may find it helpful to use the piano keyboard pictured on the back cover of this book. Which of the following intervals are INCORRECTLY labeled?

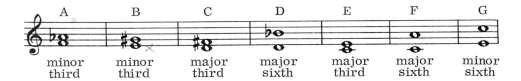

A	B	C	D	E	F	G
minor third	minor third	major third	major sixth	major third	major sixth	minor sixth

alternatives   part

a. I would like to read the background
   material before I make my choice.   258

b. Letters B and D are incorrectly labeled.   264

c. Letters C and F are incorrectly labeled.   268

d. Letters C and G are incorrectly labeled.   266

264

You're right. By counting every tone in an interval, you can ascertain whether it is major or minor. A minor interval is smaller than a major interval by one tone. Now go to part 265.

265

As was mentioned earlier, intervals of a fourth and fifth are either perfect, augmented, or diminished. Here, briefly, are the rules that determine the quality of fourths and fifths:

1. Perfect fourths contain six tones (C to F contains C, C♯, D, D♯, E, and F – six tones).
2. One tone less diminishes the fourth, and one tone more augments the fourth.
3. Perfect fifths contain eight tones (C to G contains C, C♯, D, D♯, E, F, F♯, and G – eight tones).
4. One tone less diminishes the fifth and one tone more augments it.

Which of the following intervals are INCORRECTLY labeled?

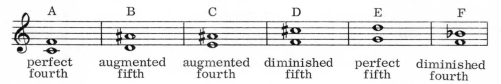

A	B	C	D	E	F
perfect fourth	augmented fifth	augmented fourth	diminished fifth	perfect fifth	diminished fourth

alternatives

		part
a.	I would like an explanation.	269
b.	Letters B and D are incorrectly labeled.	270
c.	Letters D and F are incorrectly labeled.	274
d.	Letters C and E are incorrectly labeled.	272

The answer you selected was not correct. Let's see why. Read on in part 267.

To determine the nature of intervals you should go to the piano, or look at the facsimile of a piano keyboard on the back cover of this book.

	Tones		Tones
Major thirds	5	Major sixths	10
Minor thirds	4	Minor sixths	9

Given the interval A to C♯, which is a third, you will find the following five tones therein: (1) A, white key; (2) A♯, black key; (3) B, white key; (4) C, white key; (5) C♯, black key.

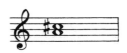

Check the table above: a third with five tones is MAJOR.

Given the interval E to C, which is a sixth, you will find the following nine tones therein, making the interval minor: (1) E, white key; (2) F, white key; (3) F♯, black key; (4) G, white key; (5) G♯, black key; (6) A, white key; (7) A♯, black key; (8) B, white key; (9) C, white key;

By counting the number of tones encompassed by any third or sixth, you can determine whether it is major or minor. Be sure to count all keys, both black and white.

If you would like to do an exercise on interval identification, turn to part 260.

Otherwise, return to part 263.

268

That was incorrect. You can find out why in part 267.

269

You can determine whether fourth and fifths are perfect in the same way you determined whether thirds and sixths were major: (1) identify the interval size (is it a fourth or fifth?); (2) count the number of tones in the interval to determine its quality.

	Tones		Tones
Perfect fourths	6	Perfect fifths	8
Diminished fourths	5	Diminished fifths	7
Augmented fourths	7	Augmented fifths	9

Do you notice that augmented fourths and diminished fifths both have seven tones therein? The difference is in the way the interval is written, not in its sound. They sound the same. Note the difference in writing in the example below.

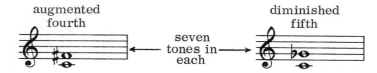

Remember that the first step in identifying intervals is to count the lines and spaces the interval covers. The interval on the left covers C, D, E, and F, or four steps. The one on the right covers C, D, E, F, and G, or five steps. Therefore, although both have seven tones, the former is a fourth; the latter is a fifth.

Continue in part 271.

No, you must have slipped up. Please read the explanation in part 273.

Use the Shield

(Remember that a perfect fourth includes six tones, and a perfect fifth includes eight tones.)
This is a fourth. Is it perfect, diminished, or augmented?

●

perfect (It includes E, F, F♯, G, G♯, and A — six tones.)

This is a fifth. Is it perfect, diminished, or augmented?

●

diminished (It includes seven tones—B, C, C♯, D, D♯, E and F.)

Now be careful! First, is this a fourth or a fifth? Second, is it perfect, augmented, or diminished? (Note the bass clef.)

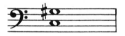

●

fifth, augmented (It covers three spaces and two lines, and it encompasses nine tones — C, C♯, D, D♯, E, F, F♯, G, and G♯.)

How many tones does a perfect fourth encompass? a perfect fifth?

●

six, eight

Now return to part 265.

272

No, you must have slipped up. For a closer look at the problem go on to part 273.

273

You can determine whether fourths and fifths are perfect, augmented, or diminished in the same way you determined whether thirds and sixths were major; (1) identify the interval size (is it a fourth or fifth?) (2) count the number of tones in the interval to determine its quality.

	Tones		Tones
perfect fourths	6	perfect fifths	8
diminished fourths	5	diminished fifths	7
augmented fourths	7	augmented fifths	9

Since augmented fourths and diminished fifths both have seven tones, what is the difference between them? The difference lies in the way the interval is written, not in its sound. They sound the same. Note this difference in writing in the two examples below.

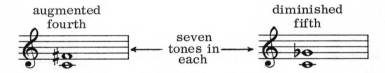

augmented fourth — seven tones in each → diminished fifth

Remember that the first step in identifying intervals is to count the lines and spaces the interval covers. The interval on the left covers C, D, E, and F, or four steps. The one on the right covers C, D, E, F, and G, or five steps. The former is a fourth; the latter is a fifth.

Now you should be able to answer the question in part 265.

Yes. You have correctly identified perfect, augmented, and diminished fourths and fifths. So far we have been working with chords of two notes only. The next step in the program is to combine intervals to form chords of three notes. Go to part 275.

If three notes of a chord fall on consecutive lines or consecutive spaces, the chord thus formed is called a TRIAD. Note in the example below that there are two intervals between the three notes in each triad.

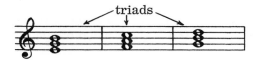

By identifying the nature of the intervals of a triad you can also determine whether the triad itself is major or minor.

The triad directly above is:*

alternatives

		part
a.	I'm not sure.	276
b.	major	278
c.	minor	280

*If you have answered this question before, answer it again and proceed with the program.

A triad is composed of major and minor thirds (which you have already learned to identify), so learning the character of triads will be easy.

C to E is a third. Since it encompasses five tones, it is major.

E to G is a third. It encompasses four tones and is therefore minor.

If we combine the above intervals, we have a triad with a major third under a minor third. This is the makeup of a major triad.

In this example, the bottom interval (E to G) is minor, and the top interval (G to B) is major. This is the makeup of a minor triad.

RULE: In a triad combining a major third and a minor third, the quality of the bottom interval determines the nature of the triad.

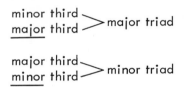

If you need to review the material on major and minor thirds before proceeding, refer to part 258 but don't lose this page while you review.

Continue in part 277.

Use the Shield

In this example the bottom interval is major, the top is minor. Which is the triad? (major or minor)

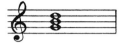

●

major

Is this triad major or minor?

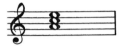

●

minor

Minor thirds encompass _____ tones. Major thirds encompass _____ tones.

●

four, five

Is this triad major or minor?

●

major (The bottom interval is major; the top one is minor.)

Now turn to part 275.

278

Yes. The chord is a major triad. If the bottom interval of a triad is major and the top interval is minor, the triad is said to be MAJOR (see example below). Conversely, if the bottom interval is minor and the top interval is major, the triad is MINOR.

major triad   minor third / major third   minor triad   major third / minor third

Now try the question in part 279.

279

Which of the following triads are INCORRECTLY marked?

1 ✓	2	3	4 ✓	5
major triad	major triad	minor triad	minor triad	major triad

alternatives

<table>
<tr><td></td><td></td><td>part</td></tr>
<tr><td>a.</td><td>May I review this concept?</td><td>276</td></tr>
<tr><td>b.</td><td>2 and 1 are incorrect.</td><td>284</td></tr>
<tr><td>c.</td><td>3 and 5 are incorrect.</td><td>286</td></tr>
<tr><td>✓ d.</td><td>1 and 4 and incorrect.</td><td>282</td></tr>
</table>

You chose the wrong alternative. You will find out why by reading the review in part 281.

You have learned to identify intervals in the preceeding pages. Look at these examples:

C to E is a third. It encompasses five tones and is therefore major.

E to G is a third. It encompasses four tones and is therefore minor.

If we combine the two intervals we have a triad with a major third under a minor third. This is the makeup of a major triad.

In this example the bottom interval (E to G) is minor, and the top interval (G to B) is major. This is the makeup of a minor triad.

In a triad combining a major third and a minor third the quality of the bottom interval determines the quality of the triad.

minor third
major third ⟩ major triad

major third
minor third ⟩ minor triad

Now return to part 275.

282

Exactly. You have learned to identify some major and minor triads. Although many other chords exist in music, our discussion is limited to these important basic ones. Now go to part 288.

283

True. Only the chords on steps 1, 4, 5, and 8 are major. Did you notice that the chord on note 8 is the same as the chord on note 1? It is merely one octave higher. These three chords are the primary chords in any major key. They are designated by the upper-case Roman numerals I, IV, and V to indicate that they are major chords. The chords of secondary importance are those on notes 2, 3, and 6. These chords are designated with lower-case Roman numerals to indicate their minor nature as follows: ii, iii, vi. (The vii chord has special characteristics that will not be discussed here.)

Question: As you know, you can form a major scale by beginning on any note and ending an octave higher (e.g., from one D to the D an octave higher, or from A flat to the next A flat). If you make such a major scale on any note, will the triads on notes 1, 4, and 5 of that scale always be major?

alternatives

part

ᵛa. yes   289

b. no   290

You have made an error. An explanation of the concept can be found in part 287.

No, you need to look at the question again. All that was asked was, "Which notes of the scale have major triads built on them?" By looking at the example in the previous part (part 288), you will readily find the answer, because each chord is identified as major or minor in that example.

The notes of the scale are numbered from left to right and from bottom to top.

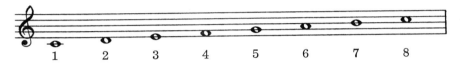

Now return to part 288.

286

You seem to be confused about something. Go on to part 287.

287

To determine whether a triad is major or minor, there are only two steps to follow:

1. Determine which interval of a triad is major and which is minor. There should be a major third and a minor third in the triad. (A review of thirds and how to tell whether they are major or minor is found in parts 258 - 262. You might review it quickly, but do not lose your place here.)
2. Determine which interval (major or minor) is on the bottom of the triad. That interval determines the quality of the triad.

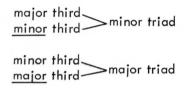

major third
minor third → minor triad

minor third
major third → major triad

Now apply the above two steps when you answer the question in part 279.

Triads can be built on every note of the scale. See in the example below all the triads that can be built on notes of the C-major scale.

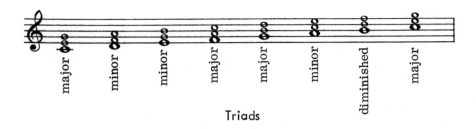

Triads

Examination of the chords above shows that the triads built on which notes of the scale are major?

alternatives   part

   a. The chords built on notes 1, 4, 5, and
      8 are major.   283

   b. The chords built on notes 2, 3, 6, and
      7 are major.   285

Certainly. The I, IV, and V chords of all major keys are major.

Use the Shield

Answer the next three questions carefully. On the staff directly below, which chords are major? Give the names of the notes the chords are built on.

key of D major

●

The chords on notes D, G, and A are major. They are found on notes 1, 4, and 5 of the D-major scale. (Don't forget the sharps.)

Which chords are major in this scale?

key of F major

●

The chords on notes F, B♭, and C are major. They are found on notes 1, 4, and 5 of the F-major scale. (Remember, the B on note 4 is B♭, as indicated by the flat in the key signature.)

Which chords are major in this scale?

key of E major

●

The chords on notes E, A, and B.

Turn to part 291.

That was not the proper alternative. The question, stated another way, was: If you construct a major scale on any given note, will the triad built on notes 1, 4, and 5 of that scale always be major?

The answer is YES.

Starting major scales on different notes does not affect the structure of chords within that scale. If the scale is a major scale, the triads on notes 1, 4, and 5 will always be major. They are therefore referred to as the I, IV, and V chords.

Return to the question in part 283.

Self-Evaluation Test

You are now ready to evaluate your understanding of the material in this chapter so you can determine which concepts you should review. When considering intervals, you may use the keyboard on the back cover if you so desire.

Match each of the following four terms with the proper definition on the right.

____C__ 1. chord

____D__ 2. interval

____A__ 3. triad

____B__ 4. harmony

A. a chord with the notes placed on three consecutive lines or spaces

B. the simultaneous sounding of different tones

C. a combination of notes that are sounded together

D. the difference in pitch between two notes played simultaneously *melodic intervals (?)*

Identify each of the intervals on the staff below by writing its size (i.e., 2nd, 3rd, 4th, etc.) by the appropriate number in the column at the left.

5 _3_ 6 _1_ 7 _2_ 8 _4_ 9 _5_ 10 _4_ 11 _5_ 12 _6_

Which of the following intervals are either perfect, augmented, or diminished?

A. second and thirds
B. fourths and fifths
C. sixths and sevenths

__B__13.

Identify each of the intervals on the staff below as major or minor thirds or sixths and write your answer in the column at the left.

14 _M6_ 15 _M3_ 16 _m_ 17 _m6_ 18 _m3_ 19 _m6_

Go to part 292.

Identify each of the intervals on the next staff as perfect, augmented, or diminished fourths or fifths.

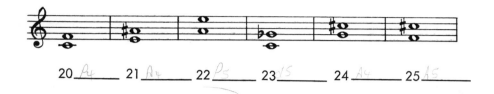

20 _P4_   21 _A4_   22 _P5_   23 _d5_   24 _A4_   25 _d5_

Pick out the two true statements from the four below and write their identifying letters on lines 26 and 27.

_B_ 26.
_D_ 27.

A. major triad = major interval over minor interval
B. major triad = major interval under minor interval
C. minor triad = minor interval over major interval
D. minor triad = minor interval under major interval

Identify each of the following triads as major or minor (numbers 28–31).

28 _M_   29 _m_   30 _m_   31 _M_

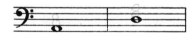

32. Construct a triad on each of the notes on the left.

_1,4,5_ 33.

If triads were constructed on each of the notes of a major scale, which triads would be major? (those on notes 1,2,3,4,5,6, or 7?)

In each of the blanks below write the names of the three notes upon which the I, IV, and V chords would be constructed.

key of B♭ major   key of E major

34. _B♭ E F_   35. _E A B_

Turn to part 293.

After checking your answers with those in the key that follows, grade yourself in this way:

28 to 35 correct answers, you have mastered the material. Review the questions you missed immediately. Then go on to Chapter 5.

27 or fewer correct answers: you seem to need a review of the chapter. Go through it again, being careful to choose your answers to criterion questions very carefully. Then go on to Chapter 5.

answers and review index

1. C (chord defined) 240
2. D (interval defined) 241
3. A (triad defined) 275
4. B (harmony defined) 240
5. 3rd (basic intervals) 250
6. 7th (basic intervals) 250
7. 2nd (basic intervals) 250
8. 4th (basic intervals) 250
9. 5th (basic intervals) 250
10. 4th (basic intervals) 250
11. 5th (basic intervals) 250
12. 6th (basic intervals) 250
13. B (perfect fourths and fifths) 254
14. major 6th (major/minor thirds and sixths) 258
15. major 3rd (major/minor thirds and sixths) 258
16. minor 3rd (major/minor thirds and sixths) 258
17. minor 6th (major/minor thirds and sixths) 258
18. minor 3rd (major/minor thirds and sixths) 258
19. minor 6th (major/minor thirds and sixths) 258
20. perfect 4th (perfect, augmented, and diminished fourths and fifths) 269
21. aug. 4th (perfect, augmented, and diminished fourths and fifths) 269
22. perfect 5th (perfect, augmented, and diminished fourths and fifths) 269
23. dim. 5th (perfect, augmented, and diminished fourths and fifths) 269
24. aug. 4th (perfect, augmented, and diminished fourths and fifths) 269
25. aug. 5th (perfect, augmented, and diminished fourths and fifths) 269
26. B (major/minor triads described) 276
27. D (major/minor triads described) 276
28. major (major/minor triads identified) 276–277
29. minor (major/minor triads identified) 276–277
30. minor (major/minor triads identified) 276–277
31. major (major/minor triads identified) 276–277
32. (building triads) 288
33. 1,4, and 5 (major triads of major keys) 288
34. B , E , F (major triads of major keys) 288
35. E, A, B (major triads of major keys) 288

5 / Major Scales, Chords, and Keys

Any discussion involving scales, chords, and keys could also be said to involve the tonality of music. An understanding of tonality requires a knowledge of the basic concepts of scales, chords, keys, and key tones – the subject of this chapter.

objectives

1. Recognize definitions of key, key tone, scale, tonality, and cadence.
2. Recall at what places in major scales the half steps are located.
3. Recall some characteristic relationships of the notes of the major scale, particularly notes 1, 2, 5, and 7.
4. Recall the syllabic names of the notes in the SOLFEGE or SOL-FA system.
5. Determine key signatures by using a "circle of fifths" diagram.
6. Demonstrate knowledge of the keys of D, B-flat, and A major as follows:

   Concerning the scale of each key:

   a. Illustrate where the half steps fall in each scale.
   b. Recognize the key signature for each key.
   c. Identify the important notes in each scale by name.

   Concerning chords in each key:

   a. Recognize the names of the chords.
   b. Identify some major characteristics of the I, IV, and V chords.
   c. Recall possible substitutes for the I, IV, and V chords.

7. Determine the seventh note that makes a V chord a V_7 chord.
8. Recall three common cadential patterns (chord patterns that form cadences).

Go on to part 295.

In order to discuss harmony intelligently, you must understand these musical terms:

1. key – any group of tones that are drawn to a central tone.
2. key tone – the central tone to which other tones are drawn, where complete repose is found.
3. scale – a stepwise arrangement of the tones of a key beginning with the key tone. (scale comes from SCALA, the Latin word for ladder.)
4. tonality – loyalty to any given key, the tendency of music to return to the keytone of a given key.
5. cadence – a pattern or series of chords that conveys the impression of conclusion.

Before proceeding with this chapter, be sure you understand these definitions. They will be required of you later in the program.

In the discussion of scales in Chapter 3, you learned that whole steps exist between most of the notes of the major scale, but that the steps from ___ to ___ and ___ to ___ are half steps.

alternatives   part

   a. I have forgotten.   Review parts 217 ff of Chapter 3, and then return here

   b. steps 4 to 5 and 6 to 7   299

   c. steps 3 to 4 and 7 to 8   297

Here is the review. When numbering the tones in any scale, it is necessary to give the key tone the first number. For the key of G, the key tone is G. For the key of F, it is F. Using the key of F as an example, the notes of the F-major scale are numbered as follows:

$$\begin{array}{cccccccc} \text{F} & \text{G} & \text{A} & \text{B}\flat & \text{C} & \text{D} & \text{E} & \text{F} \\ 1 & 2 & 3 & 4 & 5 & 6 & 7 & 8 \end{array}$$

If you examine the intervals between steps 3 and 4 and 7 and 8, you will see that a flat must be added to the B to make a major scale; however, that addition does not affect the position (or numbers) of the notes within the scale. As shown above, C is 5, D is 6, and A is 3. The identification is then very easy.

Use the Shield

In the key of A major, what are the numbers of D, F♯, and G♯?

●

4, 6, 7 (A–B–C♯ –D–E–F♯ –G♯ –A)

In the key of F major, what are the numbers of notes G, A, and E?

●

2, 3, 7

In the key of D major, what are notes E, G, and A?

●

2, 4, 5

Return to the question in part 298.

297

Definitely. As shown on the keyboard below, the half steps can be seen clearly in the key of C major, which does not use black keys. All steps in the scale are whole steps except those shown to be half steps. THIS IS TRUE IN ALL MAJOR SCALES.

C-major scale

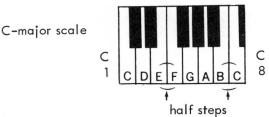

half steps

Now go to part 298.

298

In the key of C, the key tone is C; in the key of D, it is D, and so on. The key tone is always the first (1) and last (8) tone of any scale. Beginning with the key tone, the notes of the scale are numbered 1 through 8 in ascending order.

From the alternatives below, pick the one that gives the correct tone number IN THE KEY OF G MAJOR. (You may use the keyboard facsimile on the back of the book if you wish.)

In G major, the notes of the scale will be numbered as follows:

alternatives	part
a. Could I see the review before selecting an answer?	296
✓b. D= 5, C = 4, G= 1, E = 6	300
c. D= 2, C = 1, G= 5, E =3	303
d. D= 4, C =3, G= 1, E =6	301

No, that was not the proper alternative. You were asked to recall which tones of the major scale are only a half step apart.

In the following example, the notes of the C-major scale as they appear on the piano keyboard are numbered.

C-major scale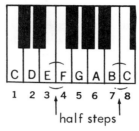

As you can see, there is no black key between E and F (steps 3 and 4) or B and C (steps 7 and 8). These notes of the scale are only one half step apart.

In all major scales, there must be half steps between tones 3 and 4 and 7 and 8. All other steps must be whole steps.

A-major scale

A B C♯ D E F♯ G♯ A
1 2 3   4 5 6   7   8

half steps

In the A-major scale, the C, F, and G are given sharps to make the appropriate half steps.

Now choose the correct response in part 295.

Precisely. In the G-major scale (or any other scale), tone number 1 falls on the key tone and the other numbers follow in order. For example:

G A B C D E F♯ G
1 2 3 4 5 6 7 8

The definition of a key tone stated that other tones in the key are drawn toward that tone. This is true with different degrees of intensity for different tones. The key tone is tone number 1, or 8, and is the "home" tone where the aural sense of conclusion or "arrival" is achieved. Tone number 7 is strongly drawn up to tone number 8, and tone number 2 is drawn down to tone number 1, as shown below.

1 2 3 4 5 6 7 8

Because of acoustical reasons that will not be discussed here, and because of western musical tradition, the fifth tone of the scale is used as the main point of departure from the key tone. Tone number 5 may resolve with equal ease either up to tone number 8 or down to tone number 1 (as shown below), falling a fifth to 1, or jumping a fourth to 8.

1 2 3 4 5 6 7 8

Other tones in the scale (tones 3, 4, and 6) also tend to follow certain patterns of progression, but the tones of main importance are those mentioned and illustrated in the preceding diagrams.

Use the Shield

In the D-major scale, the note E will tend to resolve to the note ____, and C sharp will tend to resolve to ____.

D E F♯ G A B C♯ D

●

D and D

In the B-flat major scale, which note will resolve to the B♭ marked 1? Which note will resolve to the B♭ marked 8?

B♭ C D E♭ F G A B♭
1   8

●

C, A

Turn to part 304.

No, let's look again. Go on to part 302.

When asked to ascertain the tone numbers in any given scale, it is necessary to give the key tone the first number. In G major, the key tone is G. In F major, it is F. Using F major as an example, we will first write the scale: F-G-A-B-C-D-E-F. In order to put the half steps between 3 and 4 and 7 and 8, it is necessary to add sharps or flats, but that is not needed for merely identifying tone numbers, because the addition of sharps or flats never changes the position of the tones in the scale.

F	G	A	B	C	D	E	F	Whether written correctly
1	2	3	4	5	6	7	8	(with B♭ instead of B) or not,
								the tone numbers are the same.

It is now merely a process of saying, "Which tone number is wanted"? Then read the answer. If the numbers for A and D are wanted, A is 3 and D is 6. Remember though, THE NOTES GET DIFFERENT NUMBERS IN EVERY DIFFERENT SCALE, BECAUSE THE KEY TONE IS ALWAYS 1.

Return to part 298.

303

No, let's look at the problem again. Turn to part 302.

304

Use the Shield

In D major, what is the name of the fifth tone of the scale that can jump down to 1 or up to 8 equally well?

●

A

In B-flat major, the fifth tone of the scale is _____.

●

F

In any major scale the second tone tends to resolve (up/down) and the 7th tone tends to resolve _____.

●

down, up

The fifth tone is the second most important note of the scale, only the first tone being more important. It is the main point of departure in the scale and resolves (up to 8/down to 1).

●

Both! The fifth tone may resolve either direction.

Go to part 305.

Many musicians prefer to give the tones of the scale syllabic names rather than numbers because syllables are much easier to sing. This system of syllables, known as the SOLFEGE, TONIC SOL-FA, or MOVEABLE DO system, has been widely used for many years. Most children become acquainted with the symbols in grade school. The notes are identified as follows (The scale is usually read from the bottom up, and may seem more familiar to you that way):

Number	Syllable	Pronunciation
8	DO	dough
7	TI	tea
6	LA	la
5	SOL	soul
4	FA	fa
3	MI	me
2	RE	ray
1	DO	dough

Use the Shield

The first and eighth tones of the scale are both called _____ in this system.

●

do

The fifth tone of the scale is _____ and resolves either direction to do (both 1 and 8 are do).

●

sol

In the C-major scale, the note E has the syllabic name _____ .

●

mi

In the G-major scale, the note E has the syllabic name _____ .

●

la

Continue in part 306.

306

Use the Shield

In the key of C major,
the note C would be
called _____ in the sol-fa system.

●

do

In C major, F is called _____ .

●

fa

In C major, A is called _____ .

●

la

In G major,
G is called _____ .

●

do

In G major, C is called _____ .

●

fa

In G major, F♯ is called _____ .

●

ti

Go to part 307.

By now it must be apparent that there are many major keys and scales. The diagram below depicts all major scales and the number of sharps or flats in each of their key signatures. If you begin at the top and follow around the right side of the circle, you will see that each new key adds one sharp. Going the opposite direction, each new key adds one flat. At the bottom, G♭ major and F♯ major are labeled ENHARMONIC scales, because they consist of exactly the same ~~notes,~~ *pitches* but the notes are identified by different names.

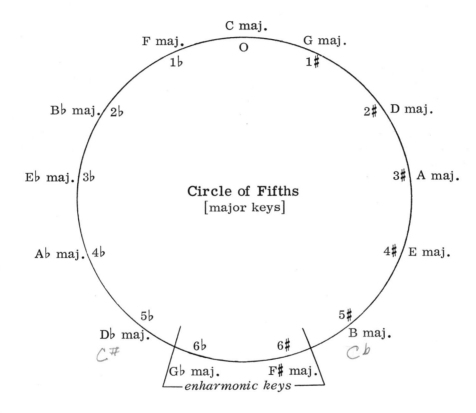

In any key signature involving sharps, the sharps always appear in the following order: F♯, C♯, G♯, D♯, A♯, and E♯. In key signatures involving flats, the flats appear in the following order: B♭, E♭, A♭, D♭, G♭, and C♭.

Turn to part 308.

308

If no circle of fifths is available, key signatures may be determined as follows:

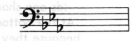

FLATS: The next to last flat in the key signature bears the name of the key. (In this example it is E♭.)

SHARPS: The key note is one half step above the last sharp in the signature. (In this example the last sharp is D♯, and the key is E.)

Here are two examples:

                                            1   2

In example 1, the next to last flat is A flat. The key is A-flat major. In example 2, the last sharp is D sharp. The note directly above D sharp is E. The key is E major.

Go to part 309.

Pictured below are three key signatures. You are to identify each key signature and choose the alternative with the correct answer. (You may use the circle of fifths in part 307 if necessary.)

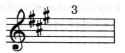

alternatives

part

a. 1 = B♭ major
    2 = D major
    3 = A major
                    310

b. 1 = A major
    2 = B♭ major
    3 = D major
                    313

c. 1 = D major
    2 = A major
    3 = B♭ major
                    311

That's right. When you are unsure about a key signature, it is not always possible (or desirable) to look it up in the circle of fifths, so key signatures should be committed to memory as soon as possible. The key signature is used to place the half steps at the proper places in the scale. All key signatures and scales are shown in the appendix at the end of the book for later use, but NOT for use during the program.

Use the Shield

In the B-flat major scale, the half steps are placed between notes and ____, and notes ____ and ____ .

$$B\flat \quad C \quad D \quad E \quad F \quad G \quad A \quad B\flat$$

●

D, E flat; A, B flat

In D major, the half steps are placed between notes ____ and ____ , and ____ and ____ .

$$D \quad E \quad F\sharp \quad G \quad A \quad B \quad C\sharp \quad D$$

●

F sharp, G; C sharp, D

In A major, the half steps are placed from ____ to ____ , and ____ to ____ .

$$A \quad B \quad C\sharp \quad D \quad E \quad F\sharp \quad G\sharp \quad A$$

●

C sharp, D; G sharp, A

The B-flat major key signature consists of (how many) flats?

●

two (B flat and E flat)

The A-major key signature consists of (how many) (sharps/flats)?

●

three sharps (F sharp, C sharp, and G sharp)

Continue in part 312.

That wasn't quite right. Please turn to part 314.

Use the Shield

The key signature for D major consists of (how many) (sharps/flats)?

●

two sharps (F sharp and C sharp)

The key of B-flat major has two flats. They are _____ and _____.

●

B flat and E flat

A major has three sharps. They are _____, _____, and _____.

●

F sharp, C sharp, and G sharp

D major has two sharps. They are _____ and _____.

●

F sharp and C sharp

A major has the same sharps as D major plus one more, namely _____.

●

G sharp

In B-flat major, the two flats are _____ and _____.

●

B flat, E flat

Turn to part 315.

313

That wasn't quite right. Go on to part 314.

314

It is not necessarily the purpose of this book to have you recognize key signatures and remember their names although it is beneficial to be able to do so. It is important, though, to be able to determine the number of sharps or flats in a key signature and to look up its name in the circle of fifths in part 307.

By referring to that part if necessary, answer the following questions.

Use the Shield

What key signature has four sharps?

●

E major

What key signature has five flats?

●

D flat major

What key signature has two sharps?

●

D major

 What key does this signature indicate?

●

E flat major

 What key does this signature indicate?

●

B major

Now return to the question in part 309.

It may be necessary to use a piano keyboard to determine the following answers. It will certainly be necessary to remember which sharps or flats are included in the keys under consideration. (The circle of fifths is in part 307.)

Use the Shield

In the key of A major, notes 1, 4, and 5 are ___, ___, and ___.

●

A, D, E

In B-flat major, notes 1, 4, and 5 are ___, ___, and ___.

●

B flat, E flat, F

In D major, notes 2, 3, and 7 are ___, ___, and ___.

●

E, F sharp, C sharp

In B-flat major, notes 2, 3, and 7 are ___, ___, and ___.

●

C, D, A

In A major, notes 2, 5, and 7 are ___, ___, and ___.

●

B, E, G sharp

In any scale the most important tone is (number), and the second most important tone is ___.

●

1, 5

Go to part 316.

So far we have identified the notes of the scale with numbers (1 through 8) and syllables (sol-fa). Each note of the scale also has a name that is frequently used to identify the chord or triad built on that tone. These note or chord names are identified below on the C-major scale. Commit these names to memory. They will be required of you later in the program.

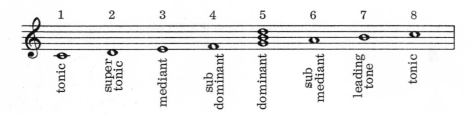

Any triad built on one of the above notes will carry the same name as that note. A chord has been constructed on G, the dominant tone of the scale. In C major, the chord is therefore known as the dominant chord or triad. A chord built on any other note of that scale will also carry that respective name. It is imperative to remember that the chord names for particular notes change when keys change. For instance, the chord built on G in the example above is the DOMINANT chord in the key of C. In the key of G (see the example below), G is the key tone or the tonic note and the chord is the TONIC chord. Although it possesses exactly the same notes as the dominant chord in the key of C, it serves a different function in the new key.

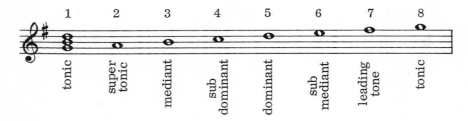

Go to part 317.

Just as the first and fifth tones are the most important tones of the scale, the chords built on these tones are also the most important chords. They are the I or TONIC chord, and the V or DOMINANT chord. The tonic chord is the fundamental chord of the key - the "home" chord where repose is achieved in most music. The dominant chord possesses not only the fifth tone of the scale (which may move either up or down to the tonic) but tones 2 and 7 as well. Tone 2 leads down to 1, and 7 leads up to 8. The chord is therefore quite dominant in its effort to resolve to the tonic. It is also the most commonly used chord for departure from the tonic chord.

In the preceding chapter, you learned that the I, IV, and V chords (tonic, subdominant, and dominant chords) are the only three major chords in any major key. The subdominant (IV) chord is secondary in importance to the dominant (V) and tonic (I) chords. However, because of its major quality and its use in traditional western music, it can be considered the third most important chord in any given key. The importance of knowing these three chords in several keys cannot be over-emphasized for the person interested in music. They are the basis of very many songs, and may be satisfactorily used to accompany the same.

The I, IV, and V chords can be determined by:

1. Numbering the key tone in the key 1, and then finding notes 4 and 5 in the scale.
2. Building a triad on each of these notes by adding notes on the next two consecutive lines or spaces.

Turn to part 318.

318

From the alternatives below, pick out the one that correctly identifies the I, IV, and V chords in the key of A major.

alternatives   part

   a. I would like to see the review first.   319

   b. I chord = G–B–D
       IV chord = F♯–A–C
       V chord = D–F♯–A   320

   c. I chord = A–C♯–E
       IV chord = D–F♯–A
       V chord = E–G♯–B   322

   d. I chord = C♯–E–G♯
       IV chord = F♯–A–C♯
       V chord = G♯–B–D   323

Review: how to identify the notes in the I, IV, and V chords of any given key.

Let's take the key of E-flat major as an example. It has three flats: B flat, E flat, and A flat. The key tone is, of course, E flat. By putting the notes of that scale on the staff below, we can begin our analysis.

The next step is to mark notes 1, 4, and 5, thereby identifying the notes on which the I, IV, and V chords will be built.

The notes in any triad fall on consecutive lines or spaces, whichever the case may be. As seen above, the I chord begins on the first line (E-flat). It will, therefore, include the next two lines (G and B flat). The IV chord begins on the second space (A flat), and includes the next two spaces (C and E flat). The V chord begins on the third line (B flat) and includes the next two lines (D and F).

Briefly, here are the steps just used:

1. Identify the key signature and put it on the staff.
2. Write in the notes of the scale and identify notes 1, 4, and 5.
3. Determine the notes of each triad by identifying the two consecutive lines or spaces above the first, fourth, and fifth notes.

Use the Shield

What are the notes of the I chord in B-flat major?

●

B flat, D, and F. The I chord starts on the key tone (B flat), as shown on the left. It includes the two lines above B flat, namely D and F.

Go to part 321.

320

That was not correct. Please read the explanation in part 324.

321

Use the Shield

 What are the notes of the V chord in the key of D major?

A, C sharp, and E. On the left is the key tone (D) of D major. The V chord will begin on the fifth tone of the scale: D-E-F♯-G-A. It will include A and the two spaces above A, namely C sharp and E.

 What notes are in the IV chord in the key of F major?

B flat, D, and F. The fourth note of the scale is B flat, found on the third line. The chord includes B flat and the two lines directly above, namely D and F.

Now return to part 318.

Naturally. By being careful, it is easy to determine the I, IV, and V chords. Here are a few more examples for your practice.

Use the Shield

In A major, the tonic (I) chord consists of _____, _____, _____.

●

A, C sharp, E (Watch the sharps!)

In B-flat major, the notes of the dominant (V) chord are _____, _____, _____.

●

F, A, C (Count up five notes from B flat and add the next two spaces.)

In D major, the subdominant (IV) chord is made up of _____, _____, _____.

●

G, B, D (Count up four notes from D and add the next two lines.)

In C major, the dominant (V) chord has _____, _____, and _____.

●

G, B, D (Count up five notes from C and add the next two lines.)

BASS CLEF

In A major, the subdominant (IV) chord tones are _____, _____, and _____.

●

D, F sharp, A (Count up four notes from A and add the next two lines.)

Go to part 325.

323

That was not the correct alternative. Please go on to part 32~~3~~4.

324

The steps to be used are:

1. Identify the key signature and put it on the staff.
2. Write in the notes of the scale and identify notes 1, 4, and 5.
3. Determine the notes of each triad by identifying the two consecutive lines or spaces above the first, fourth and fifth notes.

Let's apply these steps in the key of D major.

1. Put the key signatures on the staff: two sharps – F sharp and C sharp.

2. Write in the scale tones and identify notes 1, 4, and 5.

3. The I chord will be built on D, and will include the next two spaces, namely F sharp and A.
4. The IV chord will be built on G, and will include the next two lines, namely B and D.
5. The V chord will be built on A, and will include the next two spaces, namely C sharp and E.

Now return to part 318.

In the three columns below, the name, number, and characteristics of three chords are given. Match the items in the three columns to choose the correct alternative from those at the bottom of the page. (Your answer will be something like A-2-X.)

A. dominant

1. IV chord

X. This chord includes the key tone. It is the fundamental chord of any key.

B. tonic

2. V chord

Y. This chord is the most used chord for departure from the HOME chord. It is second to the home chord in importance.

C. subdominant

3. I chord

Z. This is one of the three major chords in a major key. Although widely used, it is not as important to the key as the chord described in Y above.

alternatives

                                        part

a. A-2-Y
    B-1-X
    C-3-Z   331

b. A-1-X
    B-3-Z
    C-2-Y   329

c. A-3-Y
    B-1-Z
    C-2-X   326

d. A-2-Y
    B-3-X
    C-1-Z   328

326

No, you have matched the wrong items. Below is some pertinent information. Go to part 327.

327

To begin with, it would be good to reread parts 316 and 317. Then RETURN TO THIS PAGE AND CONTINUE THE PROGRAM FROM HERE.

The tonic chord (I) is the fundamental chord of the key and is built on the first note of the scale. It is the chord to which most music "strives," and when this chord is reached a feeling of conclusion, or finality, is achieved. The tonic chord has, therefore, been identified as the HOME chord.

The dominant chord (V) is the second strongest chord in any key. When composers want to progress from the tonic chord to another chord, they usually progress through the dominant chord, even if they go through several other chords on the way. It is the most common chord of departure from the tonic.

The subdominant chord (IV) is the third of the three major chords in any major key. Its quality ranks it among the three strongest chords, but it holds a position below the I and V chords.

To summarize:

I is the tonic, the strongest chord in the key; built on the key tone; a chord of conclusion.

IV is the subdominant, the third strongest chord in the key; built on the fourth tone of the scale; a secondary chord of departure from I.

V is the dominant, the second strongest chord in the key; built on the fifth tone of the scale; primary chord of departure from I.

Return to the question in part 325.

Certainly. The chords match as follows:

<u>Tonic, the I chord</u>. This chord includes the key tone and is the fundamental chord of any key.

<u>Dominant, the V chord</u>. This chord is the one most used for departure from the tonic chord. It is second to the tonic chord in importance.

<u>Subdominant, the IV chord</u>. This is one of the three major chords in any major key. Although widely used, it is not as important to the key as the dominant chord.

Thus far we have not discussed the chords on the other tones of the major scale except to say that three are minor and are, therefore, designated with lower-case numerals.

Although the following generalization is dangerous because it is not always true, it is worth mentioning with caution. Each of the three major chords (I, IV, and V) has a minor substitute as follows:

chord:	I	IV	V
substitute:	vi	ii	iii

The above substitutions should not generally be made in a cadence, particularly the iii for V. Otherwise the minor chords may occasionally be substituted for, or used in front of, the related major chords with pleasant results. You will notice that the root tone of each substitute chord is located a minor third below the root of the respective major chord. The substitutes are therefore termed the RELATIVE minor chords of their respective major chords. Minor scales built on their root tones will be relative minor scales, which will be discussed in Chapter 6. *maybe*

Now go to part 332.

329

No, you have matched the wrong items. For an explanation, turn to part 327.

330

PLUS THE SEVENTH TONE OF THAT CHORD.

At the beginning of this chapter, a cadence was defined as a pattern or series of chords that conveys the impression of conclusion. Cadences are found at the end of phrases, sections of music, or complete pieces. Three of the more common cadential patterns are given below. Match the two columns and pick the correct alternative.

1. plagal or amen cadence   A. progression from V to I
2. authentic cadence   B. progression from IV to V to I
3. mixed cadence   C. progression from IV to I

alternatives

                                                   part

a. Rather than guess, I would like to read the explanation.   335

b. 1 = C
   2 = A
   3 = B   336

c. 1 = A
   2 = C
   3 = B   333

No, you have matched the wrong items. For an explanation, go to part 327.

Use the Shield

A substitute for the I chord could be the _____ chord.

●

vi

A substitute for the IV chord could be the _____ chord.

●

ii

A substitute for the V chord could be the _____ chord.

●

iii

The relative minor of the I chord is the _____ chord.

●

vi

The relative minor of the V chord is the _____ chord.

●

iii

The relative minor of the IV chord is the _____ chord.

●

ii

Turn to part 334.

333

That was not the correct alternative. Please read the brief explanation in part 335.

334

The V chord has one characteristic that bears mentioning. It is frequently referred to as the V_7 (five-seven) chord. The arabic numeral 7 is added to the V WHEN THE 7TH TONE OF THAT CHORD IS ADDED. See the example in the key of C major.

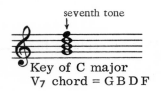

seventh tone

Key of C major
V_7 chord = G B D F

From the root tone of this chord (G), the new tone is seven steps away. When the new tone is added, the chord is known as a V_7 or dominant-seventh chord. The new tone is always added on the next consecutive line or space. Its addition increases the chord's feeling of restlessness and its demand for resolution to the tonic chord.

A dominant seventh (V_7) chord is merely a V chord plus _____.

Check your answer in part 330.

ABOUT CADENCES. The most common cadence involves the two strongest chords in any key; the V and the I (or the V_7 and I). It is called an AUTHENTIC cadence.

Another common cadence involves the IV and I chords. It is called the PLAGAL or AMEN cadence. The word AMEN is used in this description because the cadence is used at the conclusion of so many religious hymns as follows:

hymn text: a – men
plagal cadence: IV – I

Obviously the authentic and plagal cadences can be combined or mixed together for a more complicated sound. When used together, the IV chord usually precedes the V chord, thus: IV – V – I.

To review the three cadences:

V-I: authentic cadence (most common)
IV-I: plagal or amen cadence
IV-V-I: mixed cadence

Return to the question in part 330.

336

Excellent. The authentic cadence (V to I) is the most common cadence.
The plagal cadence is sometimes called the amen cadence because the word
amen is sung at the end of hymns on the chords IV-I (a-men). When the
authentic and plagal cadences are combined, a mixed cadence (IV, V, I)
is formed. You are now ready for the Self-Evaluation Test which begins in
part 337.

Self-Evaluation Test

You are now ready to evaluate your understanding of the material in this chapter so you can determine which concepts you should review.

Listed below are five terms and five definitions. Write the letter of the correct definition by each term.

_____1. key
     A. a pattern or series of chords that conveys the impression of conclusion

_____2. cadence
     B. when the tones of a key are arranged stepwise, beginning and ending with the key tone

_____3. tonality
     C. any group of tones that are drawn to a central tone

_____4. key tone
     D. loyalty to any given key – the tendency to return to a key tone for the feeling of conclusion

_____5. scale
     E. the central tone to which other tones are drawn – where complete repose is found

Shown below is an example of the G-major scale. Under certain notes are numbers and blanks. Use each blank to write the number of the note directly above it, indicating the note's position in relation to the rest of the notes in the scale.

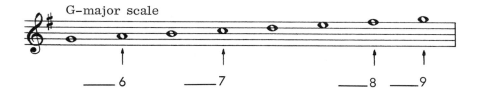

G-major scale

_____ 6   _____ 7   _____ 8 _____ 9

_____10. In any major scale, the notes are all whole steps apart except for two places. In those two places, the notes are only half

_____11. steps apart. Write the numbers of the notes between which the half steps exist in blanks 10 and 11.

_____12. In any major scale, tone 2 wants to resolve (up/down).

_____13. In any major scale, tone 7 wants to resolve (up/down).

_____14. Step 5 in the scale may resolve_____.

Turn to part 338.

338

In the tonic sol-fa system (solfege system), each note of the scale has a syllable. Write the correct syllable under each specified note of the A-major scale below.

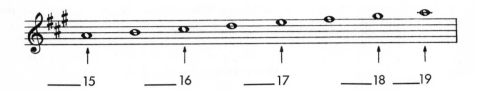

_____ 15   _____ 16   _____17   _____18 _____19

Identify each key signature below. (The circle of fifths is in part 307 if you need it.)

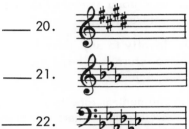

_____ 20.

_____ 21.

_____ 22.

Without using the circle of fifths, identify each of the next three key signatures.

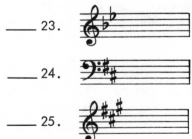

_____ 23.

_____ 24.

_____ 25.

_____ 26. In the key of A major, the half steps fall between which
            notes? (Write your answers by numbers 26 and 27.)
_____ 27.

_____ 28. Where will they fall in the key of B-flat major? (Write
            your answers in blanks 28 and 29.)
_____ 29.

Continue in part 339.

On the staff below is the B-flat major scale with chords built on each scale tone. Each of those chords has a name. Write the chord name under the chords that are indicated.

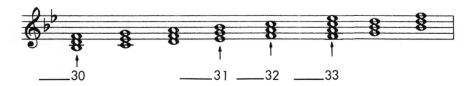

_____30   _____31 _____32 _____33

Match the next three items correctly and write your answer in the blank at the left.

_____34. tonic (I) chord

    A. The second most important chord in the key – the primary chord of departure

_____35. subdominant (IV) chord

    B. the fundamental chord of any key, toward which all other chords in the key lead

_____36. dominant (V) chord

    C. the third most important chord in any key

_____37. For the I chord, it is possible to substitute which chord?

_____38. For the IV chord, it is possible to substitute which chord?

_____39. For the V chord, it is possible to substitute which chord?

_____40. In the example at the right is the V chord of the key of A major? To make it a V_7 chord what note would you add?

V

_____41. Write the Roman numerals that indicate the chord progression used in the AUTHENTIC cadence.

_____42. Write the Roman numerals that indicate the chord progression of the PLAGAL (AMEN) cadence.

_____43. Write the Roman numerals that indicate the chord progression of the MIXED cadence.

Turn to the answer key in part 340.

Check your answers with those in the key that follows. Grade your results thus:

25 to 30 correct answers: you have mastered the material, but you should review the questions you missed before proceeding to Chapter 6.

24 or fewer correct answers: you seem to need a review of this chapter. Read it again before going on to Chapter 6. You should be able to finish much faster the second time.

answers and review index

1. C (key defined) 295
2. A (cadence defined) 295
3. D (tonality defined) 295
4. E (key tone defined) 295
5. B (scale defined) 295
6. 2 (scale tone numbers) 296
7. 4 (scale tone numbers) 296
8. 7 (scale tone numbers) 296
9. 8 or 1 (scale tone numbers) 296
10. 3-4
    (major-scale half steps) 217, 299
11. 7-8
    (major-scale half steps) 217, 299
12. down
    (resolution of scale tones) 300
13. up (resolution of scale tones) 300
14. either way
    (resolution of scale tones) 300
15. do (solfege system) 305
16. mi (solfege system) 305
17. sol (solfege system) 305
18. ti (solfege system) 305
19. do (solfege system) 305
20. E major (key signatures) 307
21. E-flat major (key signatures) 307
22. G-flat major
    (key signatures) 307
23. B-flat major (key signatures) 307
24. D major (key signatures) 307
25. A major (key signatures) 307
26. C sharp - D
    (major-scale half steps 299
27. G sharp - A
    (major-scale half steps) 299
28. D - E flat
    (major-scale half steps) 299
29. A - B flat
    (major-scale half steps) 299
30. I: tonic (chord names) 316
31. IV: subdominant (chord names) 316
32. V: dominant (chord names) 316
33. V : dominant seventh 334
34. B (tonic chord) 327
35. C (subdominant chord) 327
36. A (dominant chord) 327
37. vi (substitute for I chord) 328
38. ii (substitute for IV chord) 328
39. iii (substitute for V chord) 328
40. D (V chord) 334
41. V-I (authentic cadence) 335
42. IV-I (plagal cadence) 335
43. IV-V-I (mixed cadence) 335

6 / Minor Scales, Chords, and Keys

Although much of the material in the previous chapter pertains to minor, as well as major, scales and keys, there has been no discussion of minor keys and scales as such. The minor keys do much to enhance the sounds of music by bringing greater contrast – or another dimension – to the listeners' ears. Whereas there is only one major scale, there are three minor scales. The emphasis in this chapter will be on identifying minor keys, scales, and chords and their unique characteristics.

objectives

1. Recall several differences between major and minor scales, keys, and chords, among them:

   a. The different intervals between the notes of the minor scales.
   b. The construction of minor chords, and how the chords vary from major chords.
   c. The different kinds of minor scales.

2. Learn to determine the names of minor keys by using the minor circle of fifths.
3. Recognize the rule that identifies relative minor chords and keys.
4. Become familiar enough with the keys of C, A, and D minor to do the following:

   a. Identify the tones of these scales.
   b. Identify the i, iv, and V chords of these scales.

5. Recognize some differences between cadences of major and minor keys.

Go to part 342.

Possibly the first question that comes to mind concerning minor scales is: How do they actually differ from major scales?

Listed below are six statements concerning minor keys. Only four of the six are true. If you can, mark the four TRUE statements to find the alternative that correctly identifies minor keys.

In comparing the minor scale with the major scale:

1. The third and sixth tones of the major scale are flatted to form the minor scale.
2. The fourth and fifth tones of the major scale are lowered to change it to a minor scale.
3. Steps 2 to 3, 5 to 6, and usually, 7 to 8 become half steps instead of 3 to 4 and 7 to 8.
4. The I and IV chords become minor chords in the minor key.
5. There are several kinds of minor scales.
6. Steps 3 to 4 and 7 to 8 are still half steps in the minor scale.

alternatives   part

a. May I read the background of the
   material first?   345

b. 1, 2, 4, and 6 are true.   344

c. 1, 3, 4, and 5 are true.   348

d. 2, 4, 5, and 6 are true.   346

Use the Shield

Which tones are lowered when changing a major scale to minor?
The _____ and _____ tones of the scale.

●

third, sixth

When these tones are lowered, which major chords become minor?

●

The I and IV chords become i and iv.

How many kinds of minor scales are there?

●

three: harmonic, melodic, and natural.

The half steps in the minor scale are found between tones _____
and _____, and _____ and _____.

●

2, 3; 5, 6 (and usually 7 and 8)

The i chord in C minor begins on what note?

●

It still begins on C.

Is step 3 to 4 still a half step in the minor scale?

●

No, when the third is lowered, 3 to 4 becomes a whole step.

Return to part 342.

344

That wasn't quite right. Please read the information in part 345.

345

INFORMATION ON THE NATURE OF MINOR KEYS: In comparing major and minor keys, there are several immediately observable differences.

   1. Of the three important chords in the major keys (I, IV, and V), the I and IV become minor chords (i, iv), as does the V on occasions.

   2. The i and iv chords are minor because the third and sixth tones of the major scale are lowered in the minor-scale pattern.

   3. Because of the new accidentals in the key, the half steps are found in different places - between steps 2 and 3, 5 and 6, and 7 and 8, thus:

   4. There are three different minor-scale patterns for a composer to use: the HARMONIC MINOR, which was described above; the MELODIC MINOR; and the NATURAL MINOR. Their differences will be discussed later in the program.

Review the four points above, and then turn to part 343.

That was an incorrect alternative. Please read the information in part 345.

As was mentioned before, minor scales exist in three forms – each with its own identifying characteristics. The three minor forms are the MELODIC minor, HARMONIC minor, and NATURAL minor. On the right below, the characteristics of each are listed. Match the two columns to choose your alternative at the bottom of the page.

1. melodic minor

    A. This scale corresponds to the white keys of the scale beginning and ending on A. It has lowered third, sixth, and seventh steps when compared to the major scale.

2. natural minor

    B. This scale has flatted thirds and sixths. It contains an augmented second between steps 6 and 7, because the seventh step remains one half step from the eighth step while the sixth step is lowered.

3. harmonic minor

    C. This scale has one pattern when ascending and another pattern when descending.

alternatives

part

a. I'm not sure of the answer. Where is the discussion of this point?   350

b. 1 = B
   2 = A
   3 = C   349

c. 1 = C
   2 = A
   3 = B   351

Your answer is correct. In minor scales, the third and sixth tones are lowered; the I and IV chords become minor chords (i and iv); and steps 2 to 3, 5 to 6, and, usually, 7 to 8 are half steps. Yes, there are several kinds of minor scales.

Let's apply these four statements to several examples.

Use the Shield

To lower the third and sixth tones of this scale and thereby make it C minor instead of C major, you need to place a flat in front of which notes?

●

E and A. See the example below.

By placing the flats on E and A, we have constructed a minor scale. The i (tonic) chord now consists of which three notes?

●

C, E flat, and G

The iv (subdominant) chord now consists of which three notes?

●

F, A flat, and C

Half steps are now found between steps 2 and 3, or notes _____ to _____ , as well steps 5 and 6, or notes _____ to _____ .

●

D and E flat; G and A flat

The leading tone is still only one half step from the key tone. The leading tone is note _____

●

B

Turn to part 347.

That wasn't quite right. Please read the information in part 350.

MINOR SCALES. The natural-minor scale corresponds to the step pattern found on the white keys of the piano from one A to the next.

natural-minor scale

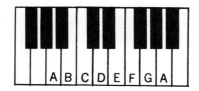

By comparing the NATURAL-MINOR to the major scale, you can see that the third, sixth, and seventh tones of the minor are lowered. That is, the sharps of the major scale are eliminated to lower the proper steps in the example on the keyboard above. The scale of A major has three sharps. The A-minor scale has none.

The MELODIC-MINOR scale corresponds to the major scale with two exceptions: (1) a lowered third on the ascending pattern and (2) the use of the natural-minor pattern when descending. For example:

A B C D E F♯ G♯ A   A G♮ F♮ E D C B A
      ascending   descending

The HARMONIC-MINOR scale deviates from the major scale with its lowered thirds and sixths. When the sixth is lowered and the seventh is left unchanged, the interval between these notes is expanded to an augmented second (one and one half steps). The harmonic minor can be identified by the augmented second between notes 6 and 7.

Now return to the question in part 347.

Very good. The NATURAL-MINOR scale corresponds to the step pattern of the white keys of the piano beginning and ending on A. The HARMONIC-MINOR scale corresponds to the white keys, beginning and ending on A, except for the seventh tone, which is raised. That is, G sharp is substituted for G to strengthen the leading tone of the scale. This substitution creates an augmented second between steps 6 and 7. In the MELODIC-MINOR scale, both the sixth and seventh steps are raised on the ascending pattern, and the scale returns to the natural minor on the descending pattern. That is to say, two sharps are used on the ascending scale but not on the descending scale. See the following examples.

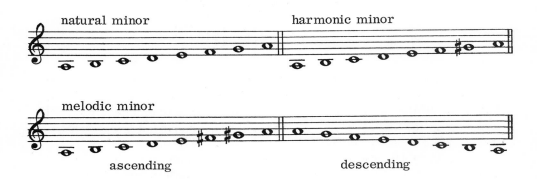

Of the three minor scales presented above, the harmonic minor seems to have the greatest use. Therefore, the rest of the discussion on minor scales will deal with the harmonic minor and its characteristics.

Go to part 352.

The key signatures for minor scales can be determined by using the circle of fifths presented below. Comparison of this circle of fifths to the one in part 307 will show the differences between major and minor key signatures.

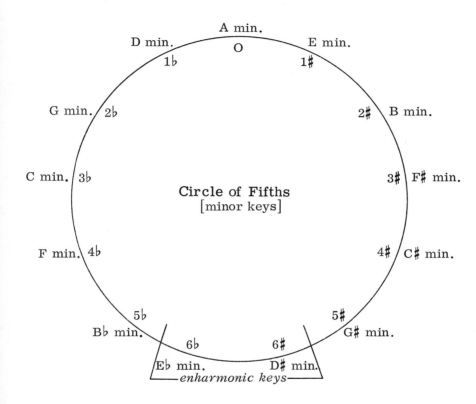

In any key signature involving sharps, the sharps used always appear in the following order: F♯, C♯, G♯, D♯, A♯, E♯. In any key signature involving flats, the flats always appear in the following order: B♭, E♭, A♭, D♭, G♭, C♭.

If a key signature involves three or four sharps or flats, it will involve the first three or four in the order listed above.

Go on to part 353.

353

Use the Shield

The key of F minor has _____ flats. (You may use the circle of fifths in part 352.

●

4

The key of B minor has _____ sharps.

●

2

If a minor key has five sharps, it is the key of _____ .

●

G-sharp minor

The key of C minor has _____ sharps/flats. They are the following: _____ .

●

three flats; B flat, E flat, and A flat

The key of E minor has _____ sharps/flats. They are the following: _____ .

●

one sharp: F sharp

The key of C-sharp minor has _____ sharps/flats. They are the following: _____

●

four sharps: F sharp, C sharp, G sharp, and D sharp

The key of G minor has _____ sharps/flats. They are the following: _____ .

●

two flats: B flat, E flat

Put the Shield Aside

Continue in part 354.

Every key signature represents both a major key and a minor key. For example, both A major and F-sharp minor have three sharps in their key signatures. When two keys use the same key signature, they are called RELATIVE keys. Thus, F-sharp minor is the relative minor of A major, and A major is the relative major of F-sharp minor. Every key has a relative key in the other mode. *not defined*

Use the Shield

If you need to use a circle of fifths to answer the following questions, do so. The major circle is in part 307; the minor circle is in part 352.

The relative minor of C major is _____ minor.

●

A minor (Both have no sharps or flats.)

The key of A major has three sharps. Its relative minor (F-sharp minor) will have _____ in its key signature.

●

three sharps as well

The relative minor D major is _____.

●

B minor (Both have two sharps.)

Both E-flat major and its relative minor (C minor) have _____ in the key signature.

●

three flats: B flat, E flat, and A flat

The relative major of F minor is _____.

●

A-flat major

Turn to part 355.

As you begin the next phase of the program, you will need to recall the difference between major and minor triads. If you are unsure what that difference is, review parts 276 and 278, and then return to this page.

C-minor scale (harmonic minor)

Use the Shield

In the above example (key of C minor), the i chord will consist of which notes?

C, E flat, and G (Be sure to watch for the flats.)

In the same example, the iv chord will consist of which notes?

●

F, A flat, and C

The V chord will consist of which notes?

●

G, B, and D (Remember the leading tone of the harmonic minor is only one half step from the tonic. This explains the B natural above.)

 The key signature at the left is for which minor key?

●

D minor

The fourth step of the D-minor scale is

●

G (D, E, F, G)

Go on to part 356.

Use the Shield

The iv chord in D minor consists of which notes?

●

G, B flat, and D

This note is which step of the D minor scale?

●

the fifth: D, E, F, G, A

The notes of the V chord in D minor are ____ , ____ , and ____ .

●

A, C sharp, and E. The leading tone must be only one half step from the tonic G. D

The V chord in D minor is (major/minor).

●

major (The bottom third is major.)

The i and iv chords in D minor are (major/minor).

●

minor

In A minor (no key signature needed) the i chord consists of ____ , ____ , and ____ .

●

A, C, E

The iv chord of A minor is ____ , ____ , and ____ .

●

D, F, A

Continue in part 357.

357

The V chord of A minor is ____ , ____ , and ____ .

●

E, G sharp, B (Remember the raised leading tone.)

Write the note names of the C-minor scale on the line below. (Don't forget to include the sharps or flats.)

(C-minor scale)——————————————————

●

C–D–E♭ –F–G–A♭ –B–C (The third flat (B flat) is canceled in the harmonic minor.)

Now go on to part 358.

358

Now that you have had some practice in determining the notes of the chords of several minor keys, carefully select the correct response below.

Which of the following alternatives correctly identifies the i, iv, and V chords in the key of A minor?

alternatives

part

a. i chord = A C E
    iv chord = D F A
    V chord = E G B   361

b. i chord = A C♯ E
    iv chord = D F♯ A
    V chord = E G♯ B   365

c. i chord = A C E
    iv chord = D F A
    V chord = E G♯ B   363

No, let's look at the question again. You were asked to identify the V chord with a raised leading tone (the capital V indicates the chord is major). Go on to part 360.

On the staff at the right are the key signatures for C minor and the key tone, C.

G, the root tone of the V chord is five steps above C. The V chord will consist of G and the next two lines above G, namely B and D. According to the key signature, the B would be flatted. But, since it is the seventh tone of the scale, we will raise it a half step – that is, put the leading tone (7) only one half step from the tonic (8). In order to obtain the half-step interval, the flat on the B must be canceled with a natural sign. The correct answer is therefore G–B♮–D.

Now return to part 364.

361

No, that can't be right. Let me show you why. Go to part 362.

362

A-minor scale

In the question, you were asked to identify the notes of the i, iv, and V chords in A minor. In the example above, notes 1, 4, and 5 are identified. The triads on these three notes are the triads i, iv, and V.

Triads:

  i: The note A and the two spaces above A, namely C and E.
 iv: The note D and the two lines above D, namely F and A.
  V: The note E and the two spaces above E, namely G and B.
      (The G is sharped, as indicated in the example.)

        i is a minor triad: A–C–E
        iv is a minor triad: D–F–A
        V is a major triad: E–G sharp–B

Return to part 358.

Absolutely right. You seem to understand the construction of chords in the harmonic minor. Next, let's discuss cadences – in part 364.

As has been demonstrated several times (parts 355–357), the leading tone of the harmonic minor is raised so that it is only one half step from the tonic. Why? As the term LEADING TONE indicates, the seventh step (TI) leads to the eighth step (DO). In order to preserve its tendency to lead back to the tonic, the half step is restored in the harmonic – and melodic – minor form. Without the half step, this demand for resolution would be lost, and the resultant cadence would be much weaker. The raised leading tone is one of the important features of the harmonic minor.

In the key of C minor, which of the following alternatives correctly identifies the V chord with the raised leading tone?

alternatives   part

   a. I believe the discussion on this
      topic would help me.   368

  b. G B♮ D   367

  c. G B♭ D   359

  d. G B♯ D   366

365

Well, you seem to be confused about something. The review that will help you is in part 362.

366

You have made a mistake somewhere. The question is explained in part 360.

Correct. You have now completed Chapter 6, and you are ready for the Self-Evaluation Test which will help you determine what you need to review in this chapter. Go to part 369.

IDENTIFICATION OF THE V CHORD IN THE KEY OF C MINOR.

On the staff at the right the key signature for C minor is shown.

The key tone is C. Five steps above C is G. The V chord will consist of G and the next two lines above G, namely B and D. However, according to the key signature the notes are G, B flat, and D.

You were asked to identify the V chord with the RAISED leading tone – that is, a leading tone that is only one half step from the tonic, or C. In order to obtain the half-step interval, the flat on the B must be canceled with a natural sign. The correct answer is therefore G–B♮–D, a major triad with a major third on the bottom and a minor third on top.

Now return to part 364.

Self-Evaluation Test

Mark the following statements with T for true or F for false.

_____ 1. Steps 3 to 4 and 7 to 8 are half steps in the minor scale.

_____ 2. There are several kinds of minor scales.

_____ 3. The I and IV chords of the major key become minor chords in the minor key.

_____ 4. Steps 2 to 3 and 5 to 6 are half steps in the minor scale.

_____ 5. The fourth and fifth tones of the major scale are lowered in the minor scale.

_____ 6. The fourth and fifth tones of the major scale remain the same in the minor scale.

_____ 7. Three kinds of minor scales are: natural, enharmonic, and melodic.

_____ 8. A minor triad has a major third on top of a minor third.

_____ 9. The third and sixth tones of the major scale are lowered in the minor scale.

_____10. Every major scale has a relative minor scale.

Each of the sentences on the right describes a minor scale (melodic, harmonic, or natural). Write the correct word in the blank at the left to identify each of them.

_____ 11. This scale corresponds to the white keys of the piano without changes if you begin and end on A. In comparison to the major scale, it has a lowered third, sixth, and seventh.

_____ 12. This scale has one pattern when ascending and another pattern when descending.

_____ 13. This scale contains an augmented second between notes 6 and 7. Step 7 is only one half step from 8, and steps 3 and 6 are lowered.

Go on to part 370.

Identify each of the minor keys represented by the three key signatures that follow. (The minor circle of fifths is in part 352 if you need it.)

_____ 14.

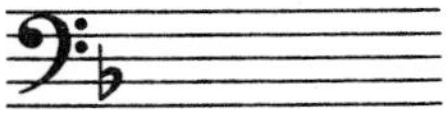

_____ 15.

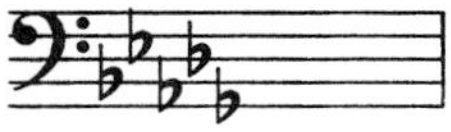

_____ 16.

_____ 17. Relative keys (i.e., relative major or minor keys) are two keys that have the same _____ _____.

_____ 18. The relative minor of A major is what?

_____ 19. The relative major of A minor is what?

D-minor scale

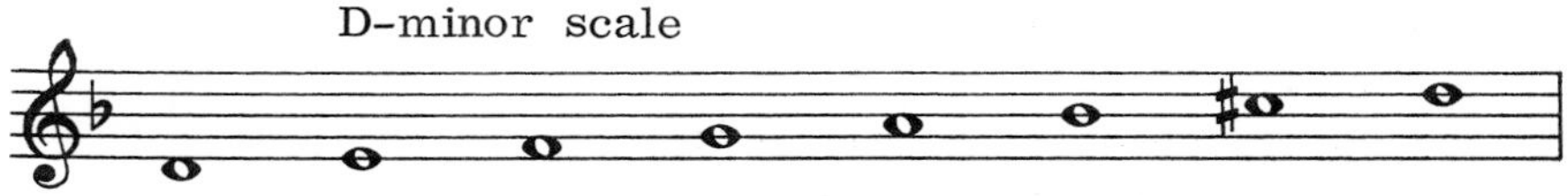

_____ 20. In the scale depicted above, the i chord will contain which three notes?

_____ 21. In the scale depicted above, the iv chord will contain which three notes?

_____ 22. Which three notes will the V chord contain?

_____ 23. An important characteristic of the leading tone is that it is only (HOW FAR) from the tonic in the harmonic minor?

_____ 24. The note G on this staff is on what scale step of the minor key represented by the key signature?

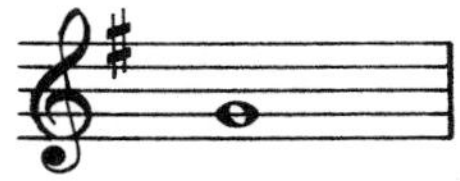

_____ 25. What chord is this in the minor key represented by the key signature?

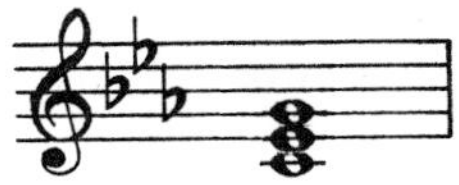

Turn to part 371.

Grade yourself on the test in this way:

22 to 25 correct answers: you have mastered the material. After review-ing the questions you missed, proceed to Chapter 7.

21 or fewer correct answers: you seem to need a review of this chapter. Read it again before going on to Chapter 7.

answers and review index

1. F (half steps in minor scales) 345
2. T (different kinds of minor scales 350
3. T (chords of minor keys) 343
4. T (half steps in minor keys) 345
5. F (characteristics of minor scales) 342
6. T (characteristics of minor scales) 342
7. F (the three minor scales) 347
8. T (minor triads) 276
9. T (characteristics of minor scales 432
10. T (relative major and minor keys) 354
11. natural (natural-minor scale) 350
12. melodic (melodic-minor scale) 350
13. harmonic (harmonic-minor scale) 350
14. D minor (minor key signatures) 352
15. B-flat minor (minor key signatures) 352
16. F-sharp minor (minor key signatures) 352
17. key signature (relative major and minor keys) 354
18. F-sharp minor (relative major and minor keys) 354
19. C major (relative major and minor keys) 354
20. D-F-A (chords in minor keys) 355ff
21. G-B♭-D (chords in minor keys) 355ff
22. A-C♯-E (chords in minor keys) 355ff
23. one half step (harmonic minor scale) 350, 351
24. third (minor key signatures) 352
25. i chord (chords in minor keys) 355ff

7 / The Structure of Music

In the same way that we could examine the tools, equipment, and raw materials used in the construction of a house, we have examined many of the materials used in the construction of music. It is now necessary to examine briefly how these materials can be put together, or how musical structure is formed or organized.

In this chapter, you will be working to accomplish the following:

objectives

1. Recognize the definitions of phrase, motive, and period.
2. Identify phrases, motives, and periods in musical context.
3. Recognize definitions for each of the following terms:
   AB form, two-part song form, ABA form, three-part
   song form, binary, ternary, free form, and round.
4. Identify in musical context some of the items listed in number 3.

The achievement of the objectives of this chapter will help to make you a more perceptive listener. It will bring insight into the constructional procedures used in writing music, and it should increase not only your understanding of the principles involved, but also your appreciation of the art form. Although it is beyond the scope of this book to deal at length with form in music, the rudimentary forms presented here will also provide the basis for understanding other, more sophisticated forms.

Turn to part 373.

On the left are three terms that describe segments of music. See if you can correctly match them with the definitions on the right.

1. phrase
2. period
3. motive

A. a series of notes that leads to, and reaches, a place of resolution or repose
B. a brief musical idea or gesture of a few notes length
C. a combination of two or more phrases

alternatives   part

a. I would only be guessing if I matched them. Where is the explanation?   376

b. 1 = B
    2 = C
    3 = A   377

c. 1 = A
    2 = C
    3 = B   379

d. 1 = C
    2 = A
    3 = B   375

Stephan Foster

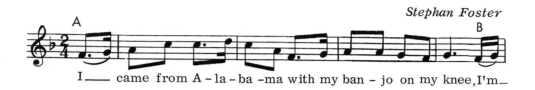

I——— came from A – la – ba –ma with my ban - jo on my knee, I'm—

goin' to Lou' - si - a – na my——— true love for to see.

Which of the following terms properly describes that part between B and C in the song above?

alternatives

part

   a. phrase   378

   b. period   381

   c. motive   383

375

You have made a mistake somewhere. Please go to part 376.

---

376   The smallest unit in music, called a MOTIVE, is a short musical idea or a gesture. It is usually only three or four notes length. In "Polly Wolly Doodle," the chorus begins with a motive:

Fare thee well,   fare thee well

The term PHRASE is the most commonly mentioned unit in music. A phrase is a series of notes that progresses to a point of resolution, or repose. In other words, it is the progression of notes from one cadence to another. An example of a phrase follows:

I___ came from A-la-ba-ma with my ban-jo on my knee,I'm___

goin' to Lou'-si-a-na my___ true love for to see.

Upon occasion, two phrases will fit together as a unit to form a PERIOD. This makes the PERIOD the largest of the units discussed herein. In order of size, from the smallest to the largest, the units usually rank as follows: motive, phrase, period.

Now return to the question in part 373.

You must have overlooked something. Please go to part 376.

___

Of course. The letters enclosed the second phrase of the song.

Use the Shield

Twin-kle, twin-kle, lit-tle star, how I won-der what you are.

What part of this song does the bracket encompass?

●

the first phrase

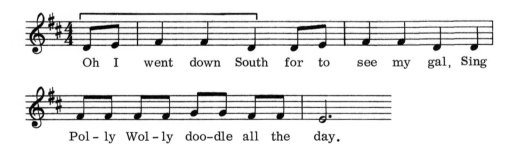

Oh I went down South for to see my gal, Sing

Pol-ly Wol-ly doo-dle all the day.

What part of the above song is enclosed in brackets?

●

a motive

Go to part 380.

379

Absolutely right. Now we want to identify these terms in musical examples. For that, go to part 374.

380

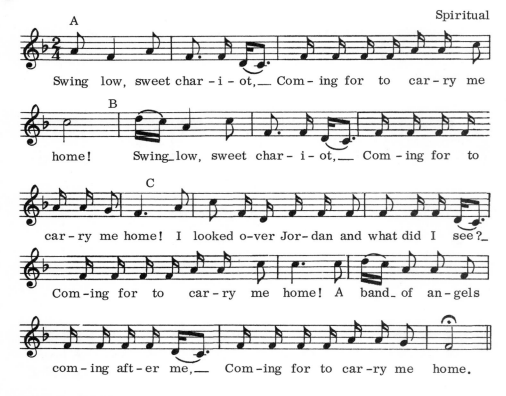

Spiritual

A Swing low, sweet char-i-ot,— Com-ing for to car-ry me

B home! Swing low, sweet char-i-ot,— Com-ing for to

C car-ry me home! I looked o-ver Jor-dan and what did I see?—

Com-ing for to car-ry me home! A band of an-gels

com-ing aft-er me,— Com-ing for to car-ry me home.

Use the Shield

What part of this song is found between letters A and C?

●

a period

Look at the same example. What term is used to describe that part of the music between A and B?

●

a phrase

In that last example, do motives exist?

●

yes, measures 1-2 or 3-4 are examples of motives.

Go to part 382.

No, you made an error. The letters enclosed a phrase, not a period.
A brief review should clarify the matter. It is in part 384.

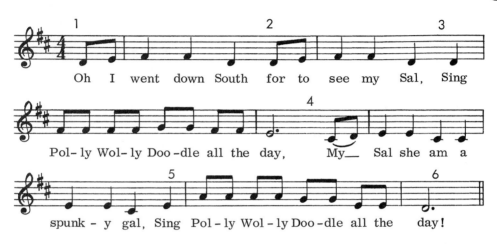

Oh I went down South for to see my Sal, Sing Pol-ly Wol-ly Doo-dle all the day, My— Sal she am a spunk-y gal, Sing Pol-ly Wol-ly Doo-dle all the day!

Use the Shield

The first phrase of this song begins at number 1. At which number does the first phrase end?

●

at number 4

Now turn to part 385.

383

No, you must have overlooked something. The letters enclosed a phrase, not a motive. Read the brief explanation in part 384.

384

Earlier in the program, a phrase was defined as a progression of notes leading to a place of repose, or resolution; and a key tone was defined as the note where the sense of repose is achieved. The song in the example was in the key of F major. The unit you were to identify ended on the key tone (F). The unit was too long to be a motive and could not be divided into two units or more (thereby making it a period). The unit is therefore a phrase. Phrases, incidentally, are frequently four measures long.

Now return to part 374.

Phrases of a song can be organized in many different ways to form different kinds of patterns.

Listed on the left are six patterns of music with a blank after each of them. On the right are four descriptions, lettered A through D. Write the proper letter after each of the terms on the left. You will have to use some of the letters more than once.

1. binary _____

2. A-B-A _____

3. free _____

4. ternary_____

5. round _____

6. A-B _____

A. A melody consisting of several sections of equal length that make good harmony when sung together.

B. A form frequently referred to as two-part song form. It consists of two main sections of music of which may be repeated.

C. A song form that follows no set pattern and is not repeated.

D. This is a three-part song form. It involves the idea of establishing a melody, going to something new, and returning to the first melody at the conclusion.

After writing in your answers, turn to part 386 and grade them. Follow the instructions at the end of that part.

386

Your answers in part 385 should read as follows:

1. (binary) B	4. (ternary) D
2. (A-B-A) D	5. (round) A
3. (free) C	6. (A-B) B

If you missed any of these answers (or if you want to read the background information on these forms), go on to part 387.

If you answered the six items correctly and do not feel it necessary to see the examples, skip to part 391.

---

387   BACKGROUND INFORMATION ON SOME MUSICAL FORMS. Probably the most widely recognized musical form is the ROUND. A round consists of several sections of equal length that sound good when performed together. An example is "Are You Sleeping"?

In this example, a first voice starts singing alone. When he reaches number 2, a second voice starts at the beginning. When the first voice reaches number 3, a third voice starts; and when he reaches number 4, a fourth voice comes in. At this point all four voices are singing – each a different section. The song may be repeated indefinitely, with all four voices singing different sections.

A second musical form is the TWO-PART song form, or one that consists of two different phrases. If the first phrase is identified as A, the second phrase would be identified as B. The form is therefore known as A-B form. Even more often the form is identified with a third name, BINARY. (The prefix BI indicates two parts.)

The form has three possible names: TWO-PART SONG FORM, A-B FORM or BINARY FORM. An example of this form is "On Top of Old Smoky."

Continue in part 389.

comma or ?
Period?

388

You chose the wrong alternative. Turn to part 394.

389

On top of Old Smok - y_____ all cov-ered with snow _____ I lost my true lov - er _____ come court-ing too slow._____

In the example above, phrase A begins with the song and ends on the world "snow." Phrase B starts with the word "I" and goes to the end. Any song that consists of two different phrases may be called two-part, or binary form.

The THREE-PART or TERNARY song form is one of the most important forms in music and perhaps the most frequently used. The word ternary means divided into three parts.

A fundamental principle of music composition is the basis of ternary form. This principle can be described with three words: establish, depart, and return; or with three letters: A, B, A. Using this form, a composer will establish a melody in the first phrase of his composition. At the beginning of the second phrase he departs from the established sound to introduce a new melody – phrase B. When this second phrase is completed, the music returns to the original melody, repeating the first phrase. The following diagram illustrates the ternary principle.

A
first phrase
(established)

B
second phrase
(new melody)

A
first phrase
(repeated)

Turn to part 390.

It should be mentioned that the first phrase of a ternary song form frequently is repeated so the form actually is A, A, B, A; but the designation is usually abbreviated to A, B, A regardless of any repetition of the first phrase.

A good example of this form is found in the French folk song, "Au Clair de la Lune."

Au clair de la lu - ne, mon a - mi Pier - rot,

Prê - te - moi ta plu - me, pour é - crire un mot.

Ma chan-delle est mor - te, Je n'ai plus de feu

Ou - vres-moi ta por - te, pour l'a - mour de Dieu.

Here, line 1 is phrase A. Line 2 is a repetition of line 1. Line 3 begins a new melody and is phrase B. Line 4 is exactly the same as line 1, and is called A' - to show that it is a repetition of A.

Thus far we have discussed three forms: (1) round, (2) binary or two-part form, (3) ternary or three-part form.

A final form, FREE FORM, is occasionally referred to as "through composed," although the latter name is not technically correct. This form does not employ repetition. It may consist of any number of phrases, each one different from the former ones. If letters were assigned to each new phrase the form would be A, B, C, D, E, etc., because of the lack of repetition of familiar material.

Turn to part 391.

Examine the song "The More We Get Together", shown below, and determine its form. Then select your alternative.

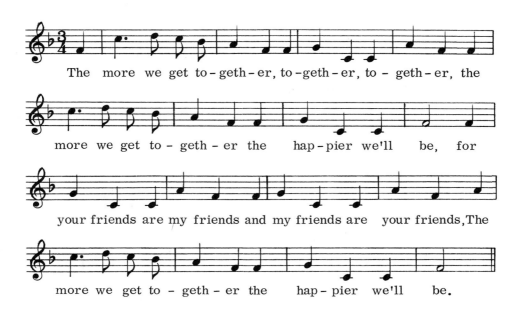

The more we get to-geth-er, to-geth-er, to - geth-er, the

more we get to - geth - er the   hap-pier we'll   be,   for

your friends are my friends and my friends are   your friends, The

more we get to - geth - er the   hap-pier   we'll   be.

alternatives

	part
a. This song has binary form.	393
b. This song has ternary form.	392
c. This song has free form.	388

That is right. The song has ternary form (A, A, B, A). Listed below are several songs that employ the forms discussed on the preceding pages. It would be beneficial for you to examine each of them to determine where the phrases are and why they are classified under that particular form.

Rounds

Three Blind Mice	Little Jack Horner
Are You Sleeping?	Sweet Silver Bells
Row, Row, Row Your Boat	Sweetly Sings the Donkey

Binary form

Go, Tell Aunt Rhody	Clementine
On Top of Old Smoky	Yankee Doodle (verse)
Polly Wolly Doodle	Auld Lang Syne

Ternary Form

The More We Get Together	Alouette
Twinkle, Twinkle Little Star	Lightly Row
Au Clair de la Lune	All Through the Night

Now turn to part 395.

You have chosen the wrong alternative. Please read the analysis of the song in part 394.

If you will examine lines 1, 2, and 4 of the song (part 391), you will see that the musical lines are almost exactly the same. All of these phrases must, therefore, be labeled with the letter A.

A	A		A
line 1	line 2	line 3	line 4

Only line 3 is different. It therefore would be identified as B. The form, then, is A, A, B, A, which is usually simplified to A, B, A, or ternary form.

Now return to part 391.

Self-Evaluation Test

On the left are nine musical terms, and on the right are seven definitions. Pick the correct definition for each of the terms.

_____ 1. motive

_____ 2. ternary form

_____ 3. free form

_____ 4. period

_____ 5. A-B form

_____ 6. phrase

_____ 7. round

_____ 8. A-B-A form

_____ 9. binary

A. a form frequently referred to as two-part song form, consisting of two main sections of music, both of which may be repeated

B. a brief musical idea or gesture of a few notes length

C. a melody consisting of several sections of equal length that make good harmony when sung together

D. a series of notes that leads to, and reaches a place of resolution or repose such as a cadence

E. a form that follows no set pattern and does not repeat phrases

F. a combination of two phrases

G. a three-part song form involving the idea of establishing a melody, going to a new melody, and then returning to the original

Go to part 396.

Answer the questions that are found below the following song.

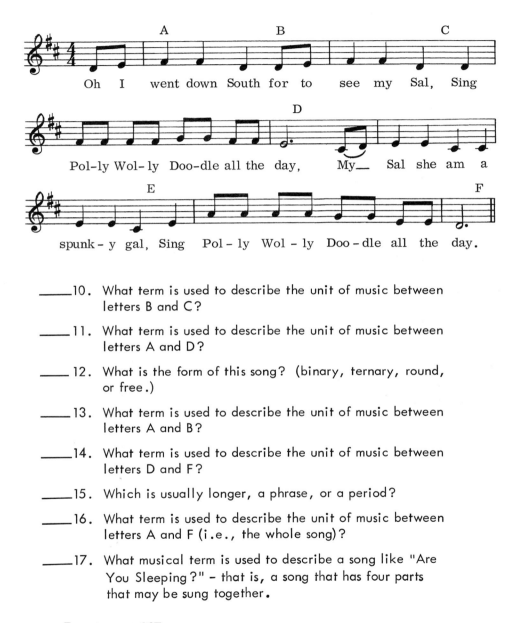

Oh I went down South for to see my Sal, Sing
Pol-ly Wol-ly Doo-dle all the day, My Sal she am a
spunk-y gal, Sing Pol-ly Wol-ly Doo-dle all the day.

_____10. What term is used to describe the unit of music between letters B and C?

_____11. What term is used to describe the unit of music between letters A and D?

_____12. What is the form of this song? (binary, ternary, round, or free.)

_____13. What term is used to describe the unit of music between letters A and B?

_____14. What term is used to describe the unit of music between letters D and F?

_____15. Which is usually longer, a phrase, or a period?

_____16. What term is used to describe the unit of music between letters A and F (i.e., the whole song)?

_____17. What musical term is used to describe a song like "Are You Sleeping?" – that is, a song that has four parts that may be sung together.

Turn to part 397.

Grading: 15 to 17 correct: you have mastered the material and need only to review missed questions.

14 or fewer correct: you seem to need a review of the chapter.

answers and review index

1. B (motive defined) 376
2. G (ternary form) 389
3. E (free form) 390
4. F (period) 376
5. A (A–B form) 387, 389
6. D (phrase) 376
7. C (round) 387
8. G (A–B–A form) 390
9. A (binary form) 387, 389
10. motive (identified) 376
11. phrase (identified) 376
12. binary form (identified) 387, 389
13. motive (identified) 376
14. phrase (identified) 376
15. period (length of) 376
16. period (identified) 376
17. round (identified) 387

Appendix

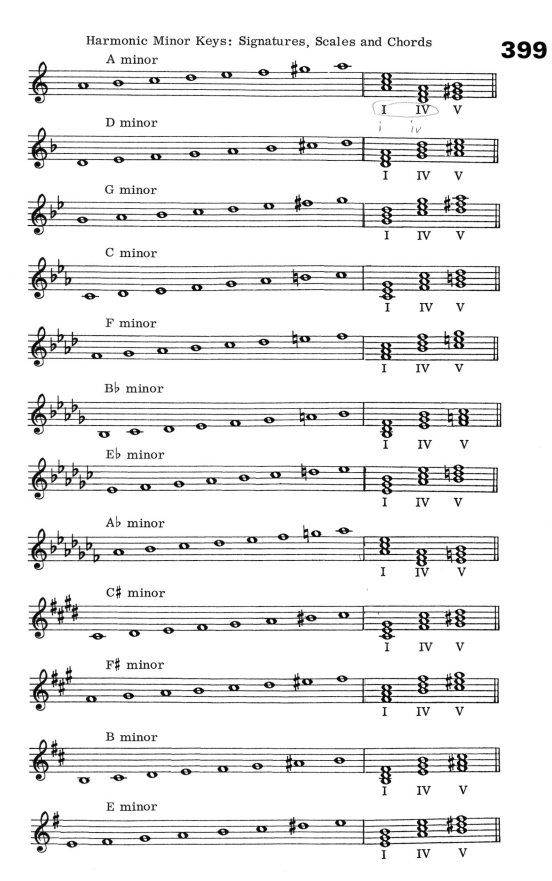

Index